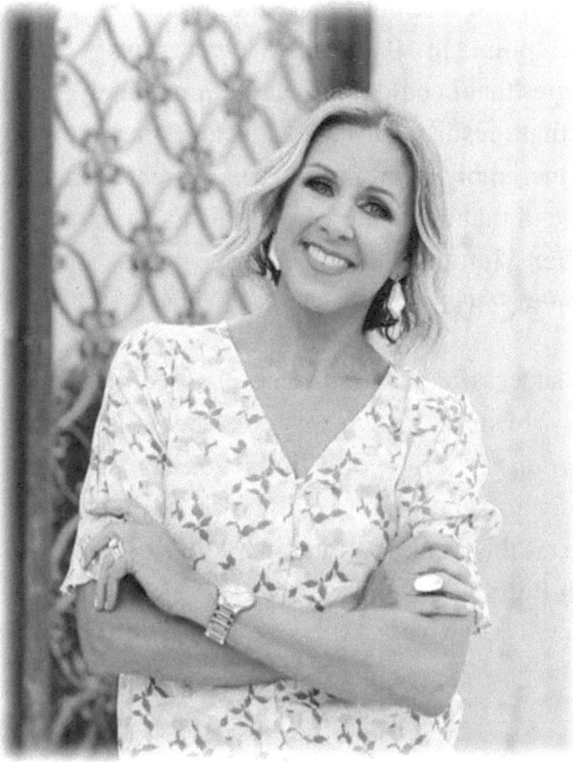

What others are saying about *Well-Oiled Operations*™

"Stacy is the queen of running a business – without all the stress! She really is the encyclopedia for the operations and strategy that'll help you thrive, and this book is exactly what you need to create the business and the life you dreamed of."
Cathy Heller
Top Podcaster – "Don't Keep Your Day Job"

"I've read a lot of business books, but this one goes to the top of my list. Like most business owners, I don't have much extra time to spend on books that talk about theory. Stacy gets right to the point in *Well-Oiled Operations*™ with steps and strategies that I could implement immediately, and I saw almost immediate results. The worksheets at the end of every chapter were incredibly helpful, plus Stacy created a quick start guide at the end that made the whole effort seamless!"
Heather Monahan
Bestselling Author of **Overcome Your Villians**

"As a successful business owner, I agree with Stacy's approach. Every business owner will benefit from *Well-Oiled Operations*™. If you find you're struggling in your organization and want to end the chaos and enjoy running your business, this book is a must-read for you."
Sarah Petty
Author of the **New York Times** *bestseller,* **Worth Every Penny**

"Stacy is a master at creating well-oiled operations and having real life success in business. This book will teach you how to do the same."

Rory Vaden
Cofounder of Brand Builders Group
New York Times *bestselling author of* **Take the Stairs**

"I thought I had a handle on business operations, and honestly, we were doing okay. However, after reading *Well-Oiled Operations*™, I see how we can make so many improvements! When we assessed where we were in our business at the end of each chapter, we could not only see that we could improve, Stacy provided the action steps
we needed to take to make our business a well-oiled one."

Jill Stanton
Founder of the Millionaire Girls Club

"Stacy is brilliant yet relatable. Building a team can feel so daunting, and Stacy does a fantastic job of breaking down how, why, and which operations can fuel your entire business and life goals and make it feel easier. Highly recommend it, especially if you have a hard time letting things go. Free yourself up. Great read."

Minna Khounlo-Sithep
Co-Founder of The Product Boss

"Most entrepreneurs start out being anti-system. They feel systems will 'crush their creativity' or 'limit their vision.' After struggling for months or even years, they finally see the light and start to realize the value of organization, structure, and process. To save yourself from ongoing headaches and further delay, you need *Well-Oiled Operations*^{TM}! Tuschl delivers a step-by-step dissection of what your business desperately needs

and offers a clear roadmap for helping you establish boundaries, clarify communications, delegate details, and codify practices, so you can get every aspect of your business working effectively and efficiently."
Joey Coleman
Keynote speaker and **Wall Street Journal** *bestselling author of* **Never Lose a Customer Again** *and* **Never Lose an Employee Again**

What others are saying about Stacy and her previous work:

"When I want clarity in my business, I turn to Stacy. When I'm feeling overwhelmed in my life, I turn to Stacy. She has this seemingly 'magic power' to make complicated things simple and... dare I say... fun. If you want to tap into this magic for your own business and life ... READ THIS BOOK!"
~ *Chris Winfield*
a.k.a. The Super Connector™

"Stacy's mind is a brilliant work of art. She masterfully articulates her systems and processes, and I've been lucky enough to experience her expertise personally. More than anything, she's someone I trust to GET IT DONE. Her conversations are enlightening, and I'm thrilled to see her sharing her knowledge to help entrepreneurs get to the next level."
~ *Jasmine Star*
Photographer + Business Strategist + Founder of Social Curator

"As a busy entrepreneur, I don't have time to read books that don't get practical about time management. That's why I FREAKING LOVE Stacy's book. She isn't content to just give you some big ideas that you've read a million times. She gives you real, concrete steps to begin implementing in your life right away. Better yet, she focuses on changing your mindset so that there can be lasting change. Many of these steps I've already started using to get more done. You absolutely MUST buy this book."
~ *Allie Casazza*
Host of "The Purpose Show"

"It's not rocket science AND it works – two things I can get behind when it comes to any strategy! Stacy's no fluff, no-

nonsense, straightforward approach to getting things done is exactly what all entrepreneurs need. Stacy gives you the direction and inspiration that you need to get into motion and accomplish everything you desire for your life. A must-read!"

~ *Amy Porterfield*
Entrepreneur and Host of "The Online Marketing Made Easy" Podcast

"Stacy Tuschl has nailed it. The first and only book I've seen specifically for business owners that's focused on our #1 problem! The step-by-step advice within will benefit any entrepreneur, no matter what type of business they run."

~ *Ali Brown*
Entrepreneur, Mentor + Founder of The Trust

"*The Implementation Code* truly IS the secret to getting it all done! It is a new way of solving a very old problem: time management. A world of success and productivity awaits those who would read this book and be inspired by it to take action!"

~ *Julie Solomon*
Business Coach and host of "The Influencer" Podcast

"This book is your go-to guide for making real progress in your existing or dream business. We all have big dreams, but the big pile of laundry or even bigger day-to-day grind often gets in the way of making real progress. We all start our dream business with the hope that it will provide freedom, flexibility, and a stress-free income. What most of us end up with is a 24/7 job that completely runs our life. I devoured *The Implementation Code* in one sitting, spent the next two days re-evaluating my business, and finally feel re-centered. Stacy shifted my mindset, gave me the tools and strategies to take immediate action, and pulled me out of overwhelm and in to action mode. If you're

ready to make a solid income doing the work that actually lights you up, this is a must-read."

~ *Britt Seva*

Social Media Strategist and Host of the "Thriving Stylist" Podcast

"If you've ever said to yourself, 'There's not enough hours in the day' or 'I just don't know where to start,' Stacy Tuschl has written the guide for you to get off that strugglebus, sister. She's a powerhouse of knowledge and has unlocked the keys to getting it all done and getting back to loving your business again. If you're tired of the hustle and the never-ending to-do list, *The Implementation Code* can get you to the other side of that hustle, and there is so much more there for you, my friend."

~ Jennifer Allwood
Best-Selling Author, **Fear Is Not the Boss of You**

"Stacy Tuschl gets more done in a day than most get done in a week – I am continually impressed with what she is able to accomplish. With *The Implementation Code*, she has created a guidebook for anyone to feel more accomplished while scaling their business. Whether you are just starting out or if you are running a multi-million-dollar company, the strategies and tips on how to streamline your days will create a strong foundation for your business to scale with ease."

~ Tonya Dalton
Best-selling Author of **The Joy of Missing Out** *and CEO of inkWELL Press*

"Stacy is a recognized business leader in both the online and off-line space that excels in accomplishing massive undertakings in minimal time. *The Implementation Code* gives you the insider's playbook on how to accomplish what you want, when you want it done, and without the stress, strain or struggle along the way."

~ Kelly Roach
Founder, The Unstoppable Entrepreneur

Well-Oiled Operations™

How Business Owners Scale Up While Scaling Back

By Stacy Tuschl

Business Coach | Top Podcaster |
International Best-Selling Author

***Well-Oiled Operations*^{TM}**
How Business Owners Scale Up While Scaling Back

Published by Victory Books Publishing
10001 St. Martins Road
Franklin, WI 53132

Copyright © 2022
All rights reserved. No part of this book may be reproduced, stored in a retrieval system, or transmitted in any form or by any means without the written permission of the publisher, except as permitted by U.S. copyright law.

ISBN: 978-0-9968104-4-9

Cover design by Jim Saurbaugh | JS Graphic Design

DISCLAIMER AND/OR LEGAL NOTICES

While the publisher and authors have used their best efforts in preparing this book, they make no representations or warranties with respect to the accuracy or completeness of the contents of this book. The advice and strategies contained herein may not be suitable for your situation. You should consult a professional where appropriate. Neither the publisher nor the authors shall be liable for any loss of profit or any other commercial damages, including but not limited to special, incidental, consequential, or other damages. The purchaser or reader of this publication assumes responsibility for the use of these materials and information. Adherence to all applicable laws and regulations, both advertising and all other aspects of doing business in the United States or any other jurisdiction, is the sole responsibility of the purchaser or reader.

This book is intended to provide accurate information with regard to the subject matter covered. However, the Author and the Publisher accept no responsibility for inaccuracies or omissions, and the Author and Publisher specifically disclaim any liability, loss, or risk, whether personal, financial, or otherwise, that is incurred as a consequence, directly or indirectly, from the use and/or application of any of the contents of this book.

*To the stressed out CEO who just doesn't know there is another way to do business. It may be the norm, but it doesn't have to be **your** norm. Here at Well-Oiled Operations™, we don't do business stressed, and very soon you won't either.*

Table of Contents

Introduction 3
Well-Oiled Strategic Planning 13
Road Map 15
Prioritization 35
Maximizing ROI – Return on Investment 45
Well-Oiled Leadership 55
Effective Team Meetings 57
Better Boundaries & Communication 69
Solid Foundations 85
Hiring & Firing 95
Well-Oiled Systems 111
SOPs 113
Delegation & Ownership 125
Leverage 135
Quick Start Guide 147
Resources 153
Acknowledgments 155
About the Author 157

Introduction

We all experience pivotal moments throughout our lives. After one happens, we are changed for good. Sometimes those moments are exciting and sometimes they're devastating, but after a while, you can start to see why it needed to happen and the ripple effect of that experience. One of those moments for me was my wedding day.

It was a gorgeous event. It's been over 14 years and there's not much I would change about that day. I still don't know how I pulled it off at the age of 23. There was an open bar with top-shelf liquor, appetizers big enough to be dinner followed by a massive buffet, late-night pizza and silver dollar sandwiches, a candy bar, and of course a several-tiered wedding cake. Everything was extravagant.

All night long, family and friends gushed over all I had accomplished and built at such a young age that allowed me to host such a glamorous celebration.

They were talking about my "successful" business.

It had been six years since I had started teaching dance classes in my parents' backyard right out of high school. I took my passion and decided to start a competitive middle school dance team called the Junior Knights. (The local high school mascot was the Knights). The first year, I had 17 girls sign up, and within three years, I had over 100 children ranging in ages from 5 to 18. I did zero marketing. Moms referred other moms and their daughters invited their friends.

Introduction

We just kept growing year after year, and although a recession had just hit in 2008, our business didn't feel it. In fact, that year, we built a new million-dollar, state-of-the-art dance studio.

From a wedding guest perspective, it appeared I "had it all."

Here's what they didn't know:

Most of that wedding was put on a credit card with money I didn't have.

I was secretly hoping we could pay it off with cash we received from wedding gifts.

Everyone thought I was running a very successful business, but what wasn't obvious was that I was the business. I did everything and held all the job titles.

I was the dance teacher, the marketing manager, the head of the sales team (of one), the finance department, the operations manager, the HR coordinator, and even the janitor when a 4-year-old clogged the toilet with too much TP.

I was under the impression this was par for the course when it came to small business ownership.

I had a mentor who said never leave a phone call unanswered or they will just look in the yellow pages (remember, this was pre-social media in the early 2000s) and call the next person. I'm a naturally very competitive person and I was also pretty broke at the time, so I took that advice very seriously. When I wasn't at the studio, I *never* missed a phone call. Ever.

So the morning of my wedding day, with my bridesmaids in a beautiful hotel suite getting our hair and makeup done, my phone rings.

Now what kind of crazy person takes a work phone call on their wedding day? Right? Anyway, the phone rings. I get a pit in my stomach and I know I have to answer it. I can't have them call my competitor; I will lose this sale. I can't afford to lose this sale, but I don't want my bridesmaids to see how sad this is. I mean truly pathetic. They'd be rolling their eyes for sure that I was so obsessed with my business that I'd even be working on my wedding day. So I quickly excused myself and went into the attached bedroom to reply as quietly and professionally as possible, "Thank you for calling the dance studio, how can I help you?"

The person calling had no idea they'd been transferred to my cell; they believed they'd called the building. Here I am thinking, "If I miss this call, I miss a sale," and it's the mom of a girl who's *already enrolled* and she just wanted to update her credit card on file before it expired at the end of the month. I wanted to scream.

I remember thinking, "It's only August 9th, why are you calling three weeks before it's going to expire? Don't you know I'm getting married?" But of course, I couldn't say that or she would really call my competitor! So I jotted down her credit card number on a napkin, (super professional, I know) and put it in my bag to deal with it later. Okay, I'm lying. I wish I could say that at least that last part was true.

Introduction

Truth: As I had the client's credit card number on a napkin, of course I pulled out my computer because everyone brings their computer to their wedding day, right? I quickly updated her card on file and then ripped up the napkin and jumped back into hair and makeup like nothing had just happened.

The videographer caught me on camera staring off in a daze and she probably thought it was wedding jitters, when actually I was thinking, "I can't keep doing this. This is not what I had signed up for."

I didn't want to pretend to be successful anymore. I actually wanted to feel it.

Now I know you must be thinking, "Should I be taking advice from this woman?"

I don't blame you. But trust me when I say that my wedding day was a huge turning point – a pivotal moment that changed my life. A breakdown that became my breakthrough.

But not before things continued to actually get worse until a **complete** breakdown finally became my real breakthrough.

At that time, I actually did have a few employees, and a week after the wedding, one of them saw what we spent, assumed I was loaded, and immediately asked for a raise. The only person who needed a raise was me!

But I didn't say that. I kept the facade going.

I would never have thought to tell her I was barely paying myself and had cut myself from the last few payrolls because we were in the summer months, and, to be frank, there was just no money left over during summer. I practically held my breath the entire month of August until September 1st rolled around when tuition came in for the next school year.

To top it all off, the only way I was actually making money was bartending. And my brand-new husband requested that I let go of bartending now that we were married. He told me he would help support us until the business "took off" and could pay me. Completely relying on him to support us financially was all I needed to light a fire underneath me and turn this thing around.

At that moment, I decided enough was enough, and I got really serious about taking my expensive hobby and turning it into a real business. At the time, the book everyone was talking about was the *E-myth Revisited: Why Most Small Businesses Don't Work and What to Do About It* by Michael Gerber. I'd read it a few years earlier, but after that day, I decided I would implement it.

The Truth Today

Now that it's been over 20 years since the backyard story all began, I've learned some valuable lessons in truly successful business ownership that I want to share with you, so you can avoid the same mistakes and be more successful and profitable sooner than I was.

Introduction

Today, I own not one but two performing arts academies (that gross over seven figures annually), and that's important because clearly, I can't be in two places at once. The business now runs *without me*. No, seriously. I went on maternity leave over nine years ago,

> **Well-Oiled Operations™ should be able to run without you!**

and I never came back to the building to work. I exclusively work from my home office and spend one hour per week on a virtual team meeting with my general manager and marketing manager. The rest of the week, I spend every working hour teaching people how I got out of the mess I was in.

Today, you'll never catch me taking a work phone call ever. Not on a weekend, weeknight, or in the middle of the work day. How did I make that happen?

To start, I have an amazing team, and we'll get into how I went from being the biggest control freak to letting other people help me in a bit.

In 2019, I was named the Wisconsin Small Business Person of the Year by the United States Small Business Administration. A few weeks after the pandemic of 2020 hit, Fox Business interviewed me on national television as a small business owner who was pivoting and having success through unprecedented times. My podcast, *Well-Oiled Operations™*, is frequently at the top of the charts, with millions of downloads. It's hard to believe how it all began.

Why haven't I let go of the studios? It's a question I'm often asked often as my current passion for helping small business owners has quickly gone from a hobby to a multi-million-dollar business. First, the studios don't need me, so they aren't a distraction. Second, I love what we get to do for our community and who we get to be for them. I started that business for a reason and it grew quickly for a reason, and I still want to be a part of that. Even if it means just popping in at the recital to watch the adorable 3-year-olds on stage or to see the 17-year-old who I can still envision as the little 3-year-old who wouldn't go on stage.

Where Are You Today?

When you put systems and processes in place, you get to do a lot more than you can ever imagine. It's actually why I wrote my previous book, *The Implementation Code.* In that book, I explain how I, personally, get so much done. Now I want to take that concept even further, and in this book, I'm going to explain how I get businesses to run like well-oiled machines.

I can't wait to take you on this journey. But first, let's identify what stage you're at because you have to know and take ownership of where you are now to get to where you want to be. We've realized that stages of growth actually have very little to do with revenue. We've seen $750k businesses that are still stuck in what we see as an early stage. Here's how I explain the stages:

Pioneer: You've got new ideas all the time, goals are constantly changing, systems are mostly in your head or you implement them in real time when you need them. There is not a lot of consistency in this beginning stage; you may be on your own or have a part-time contractor helping you. You probably don't have a ton of consistency in revenue either; some months are great, some are not. It still ebbs and flows, and it's very unpredictable.

Pathfinder: In this stage, you start to find your way, actually gaining traction. You know you've got something here – your products are more solidified, you know your ideal client, and you're starting to build out your team, adding one at a time. However, you're also starting to notice balls are dropping, and you know you have to put systems in place, but you don't know where to start.

Powerplayer: You're in the game, and it feels like you're winning, but it can also feel like you take two steps forward and then one step back. You're adding people to your team because you've realized you don't want to do this alone. You're also learning how to delegate, but you're still a work in progress. Sometimes you wish you could go back to the days when it was just you and things were less complex. Let's say, in a nutshell, "There's definitely room for improvement."

Powerhouse: You're heavily focused on transferring the responsibilities over to your team, so you can truly step out of the day-to-day operations. You focus on the things you love and let everyone do the rest; profit margin is healthy; you're paying yourself a solid consistent paycheck; and this feels like what you envisioned when you decided to start a business!

Now that you've categorized yourself into one of these stages, you're probably wondering, "How do I move up? Going from Pioneer to Pathfinder or Powerplayer to Powerhouse and higher." That's where Well-Oiled Operations™ comes in.

It's a three-phase model that you rinse and repeat over and over. As you implement the steps, you'll start to climb the ladder. As you climb the ladder, what worked for you before may not work for you anymore. This means it's time to work on the model again.

Here are the three phases:

Phase 1: Well-Oiled Strategic Planning – Gaining clarity and defining a roadmap for where you're heading and where you need to focus.

Phase 2: Well-Oiled Leadership – Building a dream team and enrolling them in the vision

Phase 3: Well-Oiled Systems – Putting systems and processes into place so that you can step out of the day-to-day operations and do what you love and/or focus on the highest paid activities…

…so that you can make more while working less!

I believe that good people do great things with money, and we need more people out there making a massive difference.

The things I'm going to teach you throughout this book are simple, but not always easy. Getting a business to run without you will take some time, but the alternative is never putting these systems into place with your business needing you every minute of the day. So stick with me. You'll thank me later when the business is running and you're spending time with your family forgetting you're even open at that time. Don't worry.

Introduction

I'm going to break things down like no one has ever shown you before. Scaling your business doesn't have to be as messy as you might be making it.

Lastly, I want you to step into becoming a Powerhouse today. Whether you're there today or not, it doesn't matter; you know you're capable of it. I want you to begin to identify as a Powerhouse ***now***. You've got to step into that identity before it ever happens or it will never happen. You don't become a Powerhouse when you hit seven or eight figures and magically develop new habits. You need to step into "this is who I am already." I am going to challenge you in this book and I want you to ask yourself, "What would a Powerhouse do?" The answer will become clear as to what you need to do next. You've got this!

Stacy Tuschl

PS. Our most successful students have their leadership teams implement all the strategies in this book with them. If you have key players on your team, bring them into this book as you read it. Create your own team book club in which you talk about what you're reading and then you can assign who is implementing what.

Phase 1

Well-Oiled Strategic Planning

Chapter One:

Road Map

"I could never do that." That's exactly what I said when a colleague in a mastermind told me I needed to get clear on my goals and be completely transparent about them with my team. This was just a few years ago after I'd been in business for almost 20 years. I was introduced to this concept of sharing goals, revenue, and my three-year vision with my entire team. My mind was blown. Have you ever learned something that completely shifts your perspective and thought, "How could I have been doing this wrong the entire time?" That was me.

Initially, I didn't believe I was the one doing it wrong. I thought my colleague was irresponsible for sharing these kinds of details with her team members. In my experience, anytime the team heard about money, usually someone asked for a raise. That wasn't just a one-time experience for me after my wedding when my team member learned what I'd spent. It has happened many times over many years.

Although I was skeptical, I am also very coachable, and I always try anything when someone who's more successful than I am is suggesting it. I decided to test this idea because I was noticing that my team was feeling daunted by their tasks at hand and my colleague's suggestion meant backing up and showing them the big picture. "They'll go faster," she said.

"They'll understand more, bring you better ideas, and the entire team will be on fire."

At the time, we could have used a little fire so I gave it a try. Let's make a long story short: it worked! I'll never go back to keeping my business goals and objectives in my mind only or listed as one of my New Year's goals. Now they're **ours**. Everyone wants to know where you're going and how they play a part in it. When they understand that, their motivation and drive significantly increase. We had our highest month in new sales and retention up to that point the month we implemented it.

But don't just take my word; here is Susannah's story:

She's the founder and CEO of Bright Beauty Collective, a full-service retail and branding agency that specializes in indie beauty brands. "Including our leadership team in the Well-Oiled Operations™ Mastery program was a game changer. I was very concerned about becoming transparent and vulnerable about our business, worried that 'if they know all of this, are they going to ask for more money?' I sat in that feeling and realized it was too constrictive. The more I brought my team into it, the more I had to trust it was the right decision and would be very healthy. One of our core values is transparency, and we stepped up communication with our contractors. It turned out that one of their big pain points was not feeling a part of something bigger, so now we do that much more than any other agency."

Start with You

Let's break down what this looks like.

One of my favorite quotes is from Jim Collins's book, *Good to Great*, all about "getting the right people on the bus in the right seats." I love that and it's so true, but when most people hear that, they start looking at everyone else on the bus and assessing. But what I want you to do first is look at ***yourself***. It's crucial to look at your own behavior as the business owner before you can identify and assess the people on your team. Most of them haven't been given a fair chance, and you need to make sure you start with the right CEO. Throughout this book, I'll be using the CEO title to mean you as the small business owner. And no matter how much improvement is needed for you to fulfill your potential in the role, you're probably not going to fire yourself, which means you're ready to commit to the work that needs to be done.

You've already heard all about company vision, values, mission, and so on. They sound great in theory, and you may even have established them. They might be in a beautiful, expensive frame on the wall in your lobby or on the home page of your website, so you've checked the box for "create mission statement." The problem is that these are almost always generic, way too broad, and no one on the team could repeat them. The bigger problem is no one lives and breathes them.

A few years ago I would have told you no one would believe in the vision like the owner. I thought, "It's not their business, so why would they?" But I was wrong.

My whole perspective changed when I was invited to Ramsey Solutions Headquarters, founded by Dave Ramsey, personal finance personality and expert, in Franklin, Tennessee with a small group of friends. One of my colleagues had a connection with someone in their coaching department, and they invited us to a private tour of their new building and to learn more about the "behind the scenes" of the company. At the time, they had about 1,000 employees and four floors. As we walked the halls, our tour guide would randomly stop the person who walked by or stop at someone's desk and ask some questions.

No matter who we talked to, somehow the phrase "disrupting the toxic money conversation" came up. Every time I heard that phrase repeated, I could feel the clarity of the common mission and the passion and sense of pride from the employees knowing the way their company impacted people and helped them improve their own financial lives. Whatever that was, vision, mission or values, I didn't care; I just wanted that. I had never experienced that before, but you know how it goes: Once you see it, you know it's possible. I immediately came home and revisited mine.

You can't just craft a vision and share it with the company once. You need to share it over and over again until your team starts using it in their own language, and we'll get into how to make that happen. But first, let's talk about the difference between mission, vision, and values.

The mission statement is what you do and who you are today. It grounds you to what you set out to do.

Your vision is where you're going. This one is least shared with team members in small businesses. Let's be honest. Not a lot of owners know where they're going, and if they do, they don't think to share it. In my business, we now update our three-year vision every year at our annual team meeting so that everyone can hear about the vision of an even bigger picture. This one is most exciting for the team. They want to hear what the business will look like and where there will be opportunity for growth.

Your values are a guide to win on your team. We use our values when we are hiring, firing, and everything in between. If someone isn't cutting it on the team, we look at it and ask what value they lack. We reward team members by explaining what value they displayed and how. Everyone on our team is extremely clear about what is expected of them.

Every Monday at our weekly team meeting, we ask someone to read the mission statement and then we do team shoutouts based on our values. We share specific situations in which our values were displayed.

CEOs are the visionaries. We are great starters but often not so great at finishing. The team has no idea where you're heading because you forgot to tell them the vision was just updated once again. Having a solid mission, vision, and values in place prevents you from often getting sidetracked by new ideas because you can assess if each new idea aligns with those foundational pillars or if you're just distracting yourself.

Most entrepreneurs are inundated with idea after idea and new visions. However, you need to slow down if you want to speed up. Your team may have no idea where you're going or how they contribute to the big picture. It's time to stop having people check boxes and start having them contribute to the conversation about how to attain the vision. If you keep changing the vision and they barely finish one project before you've switched gears, it can leave them feeling defeated. It's okay to change your vision, and possibly your mission, but don't do it so often that your team doesn't believe they mean anything and are struggling to feel like they're contributing and making a difference.

You don't have to do this alone. In fact, I don't want you to do this alone. Ask the key players on your team to share their thoughts. Host a meeting during which you brainstorm ideas and take everyone's into consideration. Decide what feels like the best first draft and present it to the team. If you've been in business for a long time and you're having feelings pop up that it would make you look bad to bring this up 12 years after you've been in business, it's okay. You're human. You can approach this many different ways. Sometimes I just admit, "I probably should have done this sooner, but here I am doing it for the first time." Or "I'll share that I've had this written down but I simply haven't shared until now and I really want to keep everyone in the loop." It doesn't matter. You can say whatever you want to say, as long as you commit to continued transparent communication.

I highly suggest doing this work yourself versus hiring someone. Yes, you can hire someone to develop an impressive mission statement and beautiful company values to display on your wall or website, but most consultants aren't going to come in and capture your culture – a critical component. I suggest you do the work and put it in your own words, then if you want to hire a copywriter or graphic designer later, you'll know it's your vision and not someone else's.

You can get feedback from your clients, too. Amy Schweiser, founder of Tiny Troops Soccer, was dedicated to giving the highest quality soccer education. She asked them questions like, "Why did you originally pick Tiny Troops and why do you keep coming here?" Amy assumed she was on track with having soccer as her highest value since she teaches soccer, but when she asked the parents what was most important to them, soccer ranked #3. She was blown away. She immediately went back and changed her website, messaging, and marketing. Her original mission statement was 100-percent focused on soccer. After getting feedback, the mission of Tiny Troops Soccer is now:

To serve military children and their friends while teaching the great game of soccer. We strive to bring a safe, fun, and playful activity into your child's life that instills in them a sense of importance, self-worth, camaraderie, and a love for soccer to carry on into every adventure where life takes them.

Building a Road Map

It can feel like an overwhelming amount of information to share with your team, and you may be wondering how they are going to grasp all of this, but don't worry. I've got you covered.

I thought the same thing too, which is why we created a one-page document we call the Same Pager™. We derived the name due to the importance of keeping the whole team on the "same page" and moving together in the right direction. I knew we needed this after bringing someone on the team and six weeks in he asked again, "So this might be a dumb question, but what is the #1 thing we are trying to sell and how do we typically sell that thing?" It was a pivotal moment for me. I knew we had too many things for sale and too many ways to sell them. He was an intelligent person who was honestly confused. I started to repeat often and remind him of what I call our Best Seller, our #1 product, and our best way to sell it. In fact, his phrase was, "The thing that sells the thing," and I liked it because everyone gets what it means. If I sell dance classes, the thing that sells the thing is a free trial. If I can get someone to book a free trial, I know that, more often than not, they will sign up for monthly classes. Showing my team a visual made it even easier.

The Same Pager™ includes:
- Goals
- Mission

- Values
- Best Seller
- "The thing that sells the thing"
- Company organization chart

That looks like a lot, right? Here's what's crazy: Without a template to follow, most CEOs typically don't even write all of this down. They tell the team once (if at all), and then expect them to know everything or be mind readers to understand expectations.

To see a copy of our Same Pager™ and a video training I did on it go to:

www.welloiledoperations.com/bookbonuses

The Same Pager™ is now your company's roadmap. It will force you to condense, simplify, and show everyone what's important as well as the fastest way to growth. More is what everyone wants, but when you look at really successful businesses, they actually do less. Doing less gives you the opportunity to do things better. If you have an endless number of products, programs, and services, it's much harder to overdeliver and master each one.

One of our clients, Lauren te Velde, from Paper Farm Press, learned this quickly. She owns a gorgeous stationery company that had over 150 SKUs when she came to us, which is very typical for her industry but still a little overwhelming. She decided to create bundles and heavily reduce the number of offerings she had. By having fewer offerings, it not only lightens your workload, it also reduces information overload for your customer. Lauren's bundles are now her Best Sellers, consisting of over 90 percent of her website sales and seven times her monthly gross revenue after she made the switch.

When we say our Best Seller, we mean our #1 focus. In fact, right now our Best Seller isn't a product that sells more than anything else, at least not yet. We are focusing on our Best Seller so that it one day becomes the best seller in our company. Tracking is imperative in business. If you want to increase something, just start tracking it. Smart entrepreneurs understand that knowledge is power and whatever you measure improves. You have to be intentional about which product you want to make your Best Seller. You'll treat it differently, and by doing so, it will quickly rise to the top. At the end of 2019, we launched a brand-new product, and I explained to the team this was our Best Seller. Month one we only sold seven. It got worse in month two. We only sold two more. However, the team was crystal clear that this was our focus, and if it wasn't selling, we needed to figure out how... and we did. Within just one year, that new program grossed a little over $850,000. That would not have happened if we didn't set and keep our intention. We could have said, "Well, let's see if this sells" and then after only selling nine in two months, we probably would have scrapped it. Does that sound familiar? Have you ever done that? I know I have many times... but not anymore.

We focus on our Best Seller by tracking our critical number every day. A critical number is simply a metric that tells you how the company is doing. Each year, we set a critical number goal for the year, and on a daily basis, we track that number to see our progress. I got this idea from the book, *The Great Game of Business* by Jack Stack. We actually track ours in units sold. We have two different levels of programs, so we want to be careful that we don't have each program weighted equally when the higher level is a three times higher investment.

That might seem harder to track, but it's really pretty simple. We count one unit for anyone who joins our program, Well-Oiled Operations™ Mastery and three units for anyone who joins our Powerhouse Mastermind. Doing this allows us to only have one focus as a team, but by giving them different values, it makes it more enticing for our enrollment team to offer Powerhouse when a client is an ideal fit.

Speaking of ideal fits, we also want to identify our best clients for whatever products, programs, or services we sell. The more specific we are explaining who is a great fit for our programs, the easier it is for our entire team to understand who we are trying to attract and retain year after year.

A lot of times, companies will develop their avatar and heavily share that with marketing and sales, but you want to make sure you're involving your entire team. The fulfillment department also needs to know who the dream clients are that you never want to lose.

We are very clear that the goal for our critical number is only ideal fits. We do not want to sell someone in our program who we don't believe will get results. Taking their money one time can hurt more than it can help. We don't want our reputation to take a hit – that our program doesn't work. Our enrollment team is very clear on who our programs work for and what types of businesses get results.

It may be time for you to do a Best Seller and Client Clean Up. That may seem counterintuitive to eliminate products and clients, but you'll find you're far more profitable when you focus on ideal fits. Ask yourself what and/or who is not in alignment with your vision, values, and mission. Do you need to end contracts or phase out certain products to only attract the ideal fits? I know you may not be able to shut off a revenue stream right this second, but develop a plan or specific phases to help you get there.

We recently phased out a program and explained to our clients what their options were as a result. They could either join us in our new program or we could end the contract and refund them. For the most part, it went well, but we definitely had some angry clients who wanted to keep paying for a program we were about to suspend. However, we knew it was the best thing for us to do as we stay true to our vision, mission, and values.

Be careful not to fall into the trap of focusing on the weak link instead of the Best Seller or Ideal Fit. I see this all the time: clients want help with the thing that isn't selling or the program they can't fill. "Oh, I don't need help with that one; we know how to sell that. I need help with this thing no one wants." Focus on the thing that everyone wants. Sell that! The same goes for potential clients. Don't go after the people who don't want your products or aren't problem aware. Go after the prospects who know they have a problem and want to fix it.

Greater Transparency

We also share our revenue goals and profit margin on our Same Pager™. Now I will say this isn't for everyone right this second; however, after reading *The Great Game of Business*, I was convinced that it was a good move for me at this time.

Owners get nervous to share the big numbers because they assume everyone will want that raise; however, this is where, as the leader, you must educate your team. I have explained to our team what our expected profit margin is and why a profit margin is important. Their pay does not increase because there is extra profit margin; their pay increases when they have stepped into another level in their role. More on that to come.

I bring this up because I find businesses put too much emphasis on gross revenue and they fail to consider their profit margin. Profit margin is actually what matters. If you're spending more than you're making, it doesn't matter if you're a six- or seven-figure business because, let's be honest, you're not winning. Most of my clients come into my program and scale revenue along with increased profit margins. But even if someone grossed less income but had increased profits, I call that a massive win. I've experienced that with the pandemic in 2020. Our dance and music school revenue dropped by about 20 percent; however, because we are a product of our product, we knew how to clean up and tighten up and get our profit margins back under control. It was such a wake-up call in overspending in some areas. We actually increased our profitability while bringing in 20 percent less revenue. As we start to scale back up, we intend to keep that profitability. I also think sharing our profit goals with the team helped them understand that generating revenue isn't the only thing we consider when making decisions. We need to know what's left over after our expenses.

I really do want to help you make more money but not at the expense of profitability and time freedom. If you don't care about that and you're just looking for vanity numbers, there are plenty of marketers out there who will be more than happy to show you how that's done, even if it means operating at a loss.

Simply put, the Same Pager™ serves as the instructions inside of a board game. It's the golden ticket that explains how to win the game. Think about it. Imagine if we were playing a brand-new game, and we took it out of the box, left the instructions inside, and said, "I'm sure we can figure it out." Without understanding how to win, you and I will be wasting a ton of time. How many people do this every day in their businesses and wonder why it feels so hard and why no one is working as hard as they are? It's because you are not on the same page… yet.

When and where should you share your Same Pager™? I suggest kicking it off at a meeting. (We will get into what kinds of meetings and how frequently you should be holding them in an upcoming chapter.)

Organizational Chart

This will be another one of those game-changing exercises if you don't have an organizational chart or aren't actually following the one you've created. One of the reasons most people are stressed is because their org chart looks like this:

TYPICAL ORGANIZATIONAL CHART

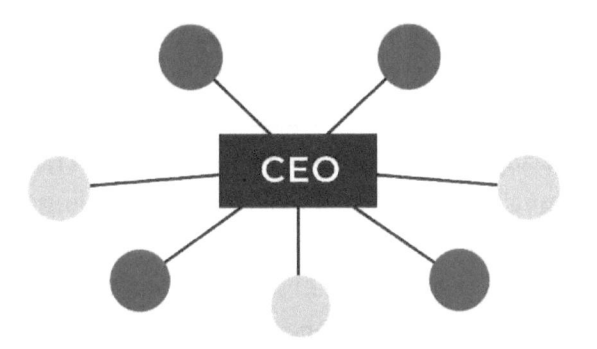

Copyright © 2022 Stacy Tuschl, LLC

It naturally happens because in the beginning when you hire your first employee, they report to you. Then you hire another, and another one, and pretty soon there are seven people reporting to you. You keep hiring, but you aren't sure when and how to bring on a manager to help you, so one day you end up like my client, Kristina Williams, from Los Gatos Elite Gymnastics. Kristina opened up her gymnastics school right before the pandemic. I would have said her timing was awful, but that wasn't the case. Her business blew up – one of the fastest success stories I have ever seen. However, she quickly found herself with 30 people directly reporting to her. I've been there and I remember what that's like. All through your day someone sends you a "quick text" or a "quick question." I love how they always say "quick" in front of it, almost as if the interruption doesn't count because it's quick, but then ends up not being quick. Am I right? Well, 30 people interrupting "quickly" all day turns into the CEO not getting anything done.

I've read all the books and listened to all the management gurus and they all agree that too many people reporting to one person is never a good thing, but they don't agree on the number. Some say five reports, others say seven, and the most I've heard is ten. Here's the thing. It's very likely that as you're reading this, you have too many people reporting to you. Most business owners solve this problem by hiring someone to be their right hand and gate keeper, and then they transfer the weight of all those direct reports to someone else. That only shifts the burden. No one on your team should have more than five to ten direct reports. I suggest for someone newer to managing people that five is the max, and you can evaluate as time goes on what works best. At some point, you may add a sixth and realize it was too much, and that's okay – you can change it then. When we get into meetings in a later chapter, we'll talk about the importance of 1:1 weekly meetings, so you see how that will start to take up quite a bit of time for your leaders. Ten direct reports means five hours/week of meetings. That alone may change the number of reports you decide is the best number.

Here is what an organization chart should look like:

IDEAL ORGANIZATIONAL CHART

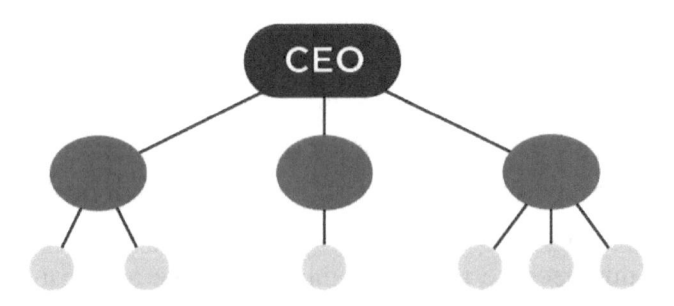

(Copyright © 2022 Stacy Tuschl, LLC)

An organization chart shows who reports to whom. When we get into boundaries and communication, we'll talk more about how to follow this and keep the team accountable from breaking these boundaries, but I want you to think about your org chart as you keep reading.

As you start to draw your org chart, you may realize you have missing pieces or people to whom you've given management roles but aren't necessarily acting as the manager. This is pretty normal when you do this for the first time, but the good news is you're reading the right book to help you fix it!

Kristina started with 30 direct reports when she first came to us, but now she only has five. Her business is more successful than ever, and she's happier than ever before. That can be you, too!

As we wrap up this chapter, I need to drive home a very important point: I read this great book years ago titled, *Profit First*, by Mike Michalowicz. It was so enlightening and I learned so much about my business's finances. I remember thinking, "How have I reached this level of success without knowing all of this?" For three years, I did nothing with that information, and then one day, I finally hired a CPA who understood the Profit First method and implemented it for me. I am telling you this because reading it didn't give me any results, but ***implementing it did***. You can read *Well-Oiled Operations™* from cover to cover. It can feel like ground-breaking information you've never heard or great reminders you were already aware of, but it won't do anything until you implement it.

That said, what I suggest is to take this book chapter by chapter and implement as you go. I strongly recommend that before you read Chapter 2, you start creating your Same Pager™. I've created resources for you as you read this book to help you even more.

Want to see our Same Pager™ with a corresponding training that goes with it? Head over to www.welloiledoperations.com/bookbonuses

Creating Your Own Well-Oiled Operation

- Create a three-year vision and share it with the team.

- A mission statement is who you are today and grounds you to what you set out to do.
- Use your values to hire, fire, and everything in between.
- Condense all these important details into your Same Pager™.
- Create your first draft of your organization chart.

I hope I've helped you understand how important your company road map is. It's about your entire team getting on the same page. Not everyone has to agree on what they think is best for the company, but everyone must agree that the Same Pager™ is where you are going and how you're going to get there.

How would you score yourself right now on your road map?
- Red: The team has no idea what our goals are.
- Yellow: Some of this is in place but definitely still have some work to do.
- Green: We are all on the same page and the company is transparent and everyone knows what winning looks like.

What needs to happen from this chapter? (Don't want to write in this book? Download the workbook at www.welloiledoperations.com/bookbonuses)

Clean up: What can we remove?

_____
_____
_____
_____
_____

Tighten up: What can we speed up?

_____
_____
_____
_____
_____

Scale up: How can we plan for growth?

_____
_____
_____
_____
_____

Not sure where to start with company values that mean something?
Head to:
www.welloiledoperations.com/bookbonuses to snag a list of the most popular company values.

Chapter Two:
Prioritization

I frequently hear clients say they wonder why someone on their team is so slow and what they can do about it. In fact, Jenny (not her real name) came to me and said, "I need to buy your program, Well-Oiled Operations™ Mastery, and I know the first thing you're going to have me do is fire Susie (also not her real name)."

My initial reaction that I kept to myself was, "It's not Susie; it's your leadership skills." I've worked with enough business owners to know how they rapidly fire off things to do, and poor Susie is just trying to catch all of the items and then magically put them in the order her boss wants. Good old-fashioned mind reading is what the boss expects and then blames the team member for being slow. "I feel like we should be getting more done" is what I always hear. While I was speaking to Jenny, I agreed she needed to jump into Well-Oiled Operations™ Mastery and suggested that she put Susie in it, too. She was hesitant because she didn't want to "waste" any more money on this person, but I insisted that she let her try it first, and then worst case, she could follow our firing system in the program.

That's one thing we do a little differently in my programs. We don't just work with the business owners; we work with people on their teams, too. We usually see a massive disconnect in communication between the boss and team members. What was really interesting during my live coaching was that Susie kept showing up and she was asking great questions. Week after week, I watched her get stronger, and I kept thinking, "How is this the team member Jenny wanted to fire?" Well sure enough, about two months in, Jenny reached out to tell me that not only was Susie not getting fired, but "Susie was on fire." She had taken off, and they were now working so well together. So what happened in just 60 short days? Let me share.

Susie was finally clear after putting together the Same Pager™ and she didn't have to read Jenny's mind anymore. She knew exactly what they were going after. However, that didn't stop Jenny from delegating way too many projects on a daily basis, but after Jenny watched our training on prioritization, things drastically changed. A lot of the time, business owners are visionaries, and they are never short on ideas. In fact, they have way too many ideas for the person who is tasked with completing them. Of course, that person is overwhelmed and seems slow. Think about it. You are constantly thinking of new ideas, and then putting those ideas on the plates of your team members. Everything sounds urgent. The new idea sounds more urgent than the one from seven days ago, so they start to reprioritize the new projects over the old, and as you keep doing this, they keep following your lead and very little gets done in the end. The worst part is you blame them. You have to imagine being in their shoes and what that must feel like. They have so many projects you've given them and every project feels urgent.

Here's how we fix that inside of Well-Oiled Operations™. We only delegate via our chosen project management software. (To view our favorites go to www.welloiledoperations.com/bookbonuses to see what we use and recommend.) A project management system is a must, but the way you use it is even more important. As you delegate your tasks, keeping them all in sections will show you how much you've delegated and what you're still waiting on. First, this is great for accountability. Second, it also clearly shows you how much you have thrown at one person. You need to get clear on what level of priority any task is before delegating it. It will help not just them but you as well. You should be the one deciding whether this is high, medium, or low and where things go in order on the projects list.

This works in other ways as well. Have you ever had a team member who always did the easy stuff or the tasks they liked the most but left the real priorities for later? Not with this system. Our rule is not to work on mediums until the highs are done. They must be done in order, and the only way to move on to the next one is when the first task is finished or they get stuck. If they get stuck, they must ask their manager for assistance, and while they are waiting, they can move on to the next project.

These two strategies alone took Susie from never finishing tasks to getting things done in the order her boss wanted. Jenny had a huge realization. She said to me, "How many people have I fired because I thought they were slow or didn't know what they were doing, but it was really just my fault?" It was a big eye-opener.

Expectations and Clarity

We forget that we are the leaders. We have to lead our teams. We have to show them how to do it, what we expect, and be crystal clear.

People want to know where they're going. When I was little and still sat in the backseat of my parents' car, I always picked the middle seat because I wanted to see where we were going. Before I left home to hang out with friends, I would ask what time I needed to be home because I wanted to know what was expected. Even as adults, most people want to know where they are going and what is expected of them, and I've found most business owners don't share this information. Again, it was the reason we created the Same Pager™. Without providing this information, business owners wonder why someone on their team just isn't working out like they thought they would.

Another way we show team members what it looks like to win is through key performance indicators (KPIs). Every position on our team reports on three to five metrics each week. I highly recommend you stick with this quantity per person. You can see how a bigger team can get more done. If you're just getting started and it's just you, you should only be tracking three to five numbers, period. If it's you and four other people, that means you're tracking anywhere from 12 to 20 numbers/week.

(To see an example of our tracking spreadsheet go to www.welloiledoperations.com/bookbonuses.)

You need to dig deep and ask yourself how any position you've created in your business moves the needle and helps you achieve your goals and vision. What activities or action items help the company hit your revenue goal? It's shocking when people tell me, "I just don't know how this person really moves the needle. Her tasks are really tedious and I can't directly relate them to our goals." Here's the thing: You either have someone who directly impacts the goals or you have someone taking things off your plate (or a leader's plate), so you can directly impact the goals even more. It has to be that simple.

Here's where most business owners go wrong. For example, they believe they must post on social media every day because that's what they've been told. So they hire a social media manager and they have as their KPI to post daily on social. Let's be real. How many times have you posted on social media just to check it off your list and nothing happened? No leads, no sales, just a like or two that didn't do anything for you, if you're being honest.

In my children's dance and music schools, I know if potential clients sign up for a free trial, we have a 90-percent-plus close rate if they show up in the studio. My social media manager has a KPI of booking trials from social platforms. Instead of thinking, "I need to post on social today," she thinks, "How can I post and get someone to book a free trial?" Imagine what happens when your social media manager now realizes the real goal of her job? It's a minor shift with a massive difference. I work with a lot of clients who have too many team members with fluffy KPIs and they have no idea if they are getting a return on investment with that position because they aren't tracking the right things.

Don't know what numbers to start tracking? Get the book, *Key Performance Indicators (KPI): The 75 measures every manager needs to know* by Bernard Marr. You won't necessarily read this book, but you'll use it to reference what you could track. He separates metrics by each department, and it's a great guide if you're unsure. Remember, you only get to pick three to five per team member. Another way to pick your KPIs is to explain this to your team and see what they think they should be shooting for. The idea is that these KPIs would – and should – make a difference on the bottom line. If KPIs started to grow, the company would grow. Once you explain that, your team may start to share what they are doing that is really important. Don't forget that if you realize a lot of your team members haven't been doing productive tasks, you are the leader. Please don't immediately go into the blame game. Fix it and start fresh.

As they begin to report, you'll start to see trends. Every week use these numbers to get curious. Why is this increasing? How can we do even more of that? Why did this number drastically go down? What did we do? What did we not do? This is how you know if the business is winning or not and you start to uncover which actions are working and which aren't.

Each person on your team will have daily, weekly, monthly, quarterly, and annual routines. These are things that must be done to ensure consistent growth of your business. However, a project is a one-time thing. A routine might be every Thursday to send out the weekly newsletter to clients but a project might be rebranding your website. I have seen over and over again that team members can get overwhelmed and not know what to do first. You want to make sure your team is aware of their routines being priority unless they hear otherwise. Projects are only worked on when routines are done.

If you stopped reading here and put Chapters 1 and 2 into place, your business would probably start to become unrecognizable as the issues that caused friction and problems become more well-oiled and running smoother than you ever experienced. Of course, I want you to keep reading the rest of this book because we are just getting started, but remember that reading is just one piece of the puzzle. You need to read it to understand, but *you need to implement it to get results*. Don't forget that.

Creating Your Own Well-Oiled Operation

- Prioritization must start with the leader.
- Project management systems are a must, but you must use them strategically for them to work.
- Each team member, including the owner, has three to five KPIs.

Prioritization

- KPIs should be reported on a weekly basis.
- Make sure every team member understands their routines and that they take priority over projects.

How would you score yourself right now on prioritization?
- Red: No prioritization or KPIs.
- Yellow: Some of this is in place but definitely still have some work to do.
- Green: Everyone knows what to do in order of priority, and all tasks have due dates/deadlines on them, and KPIs are set with weekly reporting in place.

What needs to happen from this chapter? (Don't want to write in this book, download the workbook at www.welloiledoperations.com/bookbonuses)

Clean up: What can we remove?
_____
_____
_____
_____

Tighten up: What can we speed up?

_____
_____
_____
_____
_____

Scale up: How can we plan for growth?

_____
_____
_____
_____
_____

To see what project management software we recommend and for a quick video demonstration of how we use it to help prioritize, go to:

www.welloiledoperations.com/bookbonuses.

Prioritization

Chapter Three:
Maximizing ROI – Return on Investment

When people hear about my coaching and consulting and discussions of creating Well-Oiled Operations™, they immediately think I'm going to push them to hire more team members. No, that is not at all where I start. That would only add to the chaos they are probably already experiencing, and that's never the right solution for any problem.

Let me share an example: Have you ever seen one of the gorgeous closets organized by *The Home Edit*? Everything is perfectly displayed in a spot designed exactly for that item. It's wonderful; however, if you've ever watched the show on Netflix, you know it takes several steps to achieve the end result, and in fact, it gets ***even messier before it begins to get better***. They toss, donate, and only keep what lights them up – the typical steps to decluttering. You don't buy anything new (a.k.a. a new hire) until you've gone through the process of reducing the clutter (a.k.a. the chaos).

This is how I want you to think about your team. When starting to improve your operation to make it a well-oiled one, usually you want to avoid hiring immediately because you have some clean up to do first. You want to make sure everyone is staying in your business and that they are maximized and working efficiently before you add anyone new.

I recently coached a client inside Well-Oiled Operations™ Mastery who realized she needed two additional people, but she was worried about her current finances. Shelby Grassman owns Lakeside Restaurant, Motel, and RV Park in Christmas Valley, OR. I did a little digging, and we realized that what she wanted to accomplish with these two new positions could actually be done by her current team members. She wanted to hire a social media manager. Social media always felt like a big project and took so much time. On the restaurant side, she uses one of her perfectly plated dishes as a showcase. She's a busy entrepreneur and simply didn't have the time. Even with a social media manager, she would still be the one to cook, design, and take the photo. She's a talented photographer, and that's part of the reason her posts (when she has time for them) do so well on social media. What she really needed was someone to handle the posting.

We discussed the burden of the constant need to prepare a dish, photograph it, and post on an ongoing basis. I helped her develop a schedule of setting aside one day (or part of one day) to prepare and photograph several dishes that could then be dripped out on social media. We created a content bank of all the images, so the task could be turned over to someone else to actually create and schedule the posts. Once we discovered this efficiency strategy for her, we realized there would not be enough left to do to warrant hiring someone. Shelby was able to assign this to someone on her current team. This is what I mean by maximizing efficiencies before adding to the chaos.

Questions to Ask

When it comes to assigning tasks to reduce the chaos, the first step is to assess who's on your team now. I learned a great way to go about that from the book, *Traction: Get a Grip on Your Business* by Gino Wickman. It's the GWC method, and it involves three steps:

1. G: Do they **get** it?
2. W: Do they **want** it?
3. C: Are they **capable**?

In the first step, you must assess if your team member understands what you're asking, not only in terms of the task but also how it relates to the big picture of your vision.

Do they want it? You need to know that the task you want to assign really lights them up – is this something they'll be passionate about – rather than simply another item on their to-do list.

Finally, are they capable of carrying it out? Does it fall within their current skillset? If not, is it something they can (and are willing to) learn?

You want to make sure each person on your team has all three for whatever their job function happens to be. I've been in business long enough to know that you probably have people on your team who do **not** have all three. If someone is missing one of the elements, you need to address it. I'm sure it's contributing to the chaos. I have directly asked people: Do you want to work here? Do you love your job? I've had people fight and insist they love working for me and what they're doing. Okay, great. Now I see they want it, so what's the problem? Either they're not understanding what I'm asking or are incapable.

If you create a better, more detailed system for them to follow and they still can't do it, they are just not capable. But… can they learn? Some may and some may not. For those who can't learn the task, you'll have to determine whether there is a different role for them or let them go. Let me warn you: Do not find a role for them simply because you don't want to fire. I've been down that road. I hired someone for office and admin work, and I quickly learned she'd exaggerated on her tech savviness. I started to find other jobs for her to do to keep her busy, but I soon became resentful. I hired her for one thing, and now I was paying her to do things that I didn't really need done. Eventually, I had to let her go. Firing is never fun, but you have a business to run, and if you want to be like other Well-Oiled Operations™, it's a strategy you'll need to learn and master. (Don't worry, we're going to cover this in an upcoming chapter.)

Firing can be a good thing because you make room for a better fit. When you clean up the bottom, you make room for your team to rise to the top. Once you learn how this works and the power of delegation – and how much easier it is to run a business with a team – it can get addicting. You'll become a hiring machine; however, as that is happening, you must know how much of your overhead can be allocated to labor. It's different industry by industry, so talk to your CPA about what makes sense for your particular industry and business. Use that number to assess your current situation. If the goal is no more than 30 percent labor-to-revenue, and you're at 25 percent, you have a little room to hire. If you're at 30 percent but really feel like you need to hire someone, you must first ensure you're maximizing everyone on your team right now. Once you've done that, develop a plan to increase revenue and profits first, and as soon as you create a little wiggle room on your labor percentage, then go for it.

Tightening Up the Team

I was recently at my goal for percentage of labor, but I felt the team was maxed out. I was pretty sure we could not grow without bringing on a new hire, so here's what I did: I applied the 80/20 rule. As a quick sidebar, the 80/20 rule (also known as the Pareto Principle, named for economist Vilfredo Pareto) asserts that 80 percent of outcomes result from 20 percent of causes or inputs. I figured that each person on my team was getting 80 percent of their results from 20 percent of their activities, so I decided to challenge them on one of their weekly tasks. I wanted to know what they believed were the least effective tasks they were doing. I wanted five hours shaved off their plate, and the only rule for doing this was that it couldn't cost us money or negatively impact our current clients. Everyone on the team brainstormed about what they could remove.

From there, I reviewed and found inefficiencies. There were some really great ideas. People felt confident to say, "I do this every week, but I don't think anyone is doing anything with the information." Talk about a waste of time. I was actually shocked to hear about some tasks for which my own response was, "You're still doing that?" As business owners, we all assign things to people and then forget we did, but months after the fact, they're still doing it because you'd assigned it. We tallied up many wasted hours from this exercise. At the time, I had ten people on the team, and we found a total of 50 hours freed up. Right there was the room I needed to hire another person, and the best part was it didn't cost me a dollar. It was all about maximizing!

What did we do with that extra time for my existing team members? Before I chimed in with any new ideas, I asked them, "What do you think is your highest-producing task each week? What positively impacts our customers or generates the most revenue?"

> *The real beauty is this becomes a never-ending cycle. You hire, maximize your team, the business grows, then you hire again, maximize again, and grow again.*

As entrepreneurs, we always have a million new ideas that may – or may not – work. However, when you pour extra fuel on the fire of what's already working, you'll be able to generate so much more and do so much faster. Here's the best part of having your team refocus to think about revenue generation and positive customer impacts: The business will feel the shift, and after implementing, you'll generate the revenue to justify the new hire you want.

If you're like Shelby and have new tasks (or tasks you want off your own plate) and would like to delegate, just ask. See if they want to try a few hours each week and determine how they do, keeping GWC in mind. They may be a temporary fill-in until you can afford to hire or it may turn out that a few hours is all that's needed and, voilà, you have your solution.

Before you ever hire anyone new, make sure to offer more work to any part-time rocks stars on your team. It's so much easier to add to someone's existing plate who's great on your team than it is to start training someone new. I've learned that the more I give my part-timers and the longer they work on our team, the more committed they become and the more our business becomes their #1 priority. When someone only works 10 to 15 hours and has another job, wherever they spend more time trumps everything else. That said, if you're a part-timer's #2 priority right now, that doesn't mean it can't change. We recently made a full-time offer to someone for whom we were #2, and they jumped at it. Honestly, it was someone I never thought would fully leave the other company, but they saw the opportunity and took it.

The bottom line (literally and figuratively) is that labor is going to be one of your biggest monthly expenses. Most business owners try to solve problems (and reduce chaos) by making another hire. However, they haven't maximized everyone on their team, so they're only making all the problems worse while eating away at profit.

One of my favorite ways to prove this is by having team members do time audits every 90 days. We use a spreadsheet to track how much time is spent on projects versus daily routines. Every 90 days, we get a pulse on what each team member is doing, how long it's taking, and then determine if we're getting an ROI on that activity. Remove tasks that don't produce an ROI and make your team stronger every 90 days.

For example, once you see a specific task takes seven hours/week by someone making $25/hour, you can ask if you're seeing a $175 return every single week. It quickly becomes obvious when something is working or not when you do this math. You'll then either modify the task or delete it if it's not producing a return. If it is, you may want to put even more energy and attention into that activity.

How much money are you wasting on your current payroll because your team isn't maximized?

Creating Your Own Well-Oiled Operation

- Assess each person on your team. Do they get to stay?
- Assign the 5-Hour Challenge (80/20 rule: Have them figure out where they can carve five hours out of their weekly schedule).
- Get rid of those five hours and replace them with more of what's working and getting results.
- Before you hire, offer more hours to part-time positions.
- Incorporate time audits every 90 days.

Well-Oiled Operations™

How would you score yourself right now on maximizing?

- Red: No idea if your team members are maxed out or you know they aren't 100%.
- Yellow: Some of this is in place but definitely still have some work to do.
- Green: Everyone is effective and efficient and working on things that produce an ROI.

What needs to happen from this chapter? (Don't want to write in this book, download the workbook at www.welloiledoperations.com/bookbonuses)

Clean up: What can we remove?

_____
_____
_____
_____

Tighten up: What can we speed up?

_____
_____
_____
_____

Scale up: How can we plan for growth?

_____
_____
_____
_____
_____

To get complete details on the 5-Hour Challenge, go to www.welloiledoperations.com/bookbonuses.

Phase 2

Well-Oiled Leadership

Chapter Four:
Effective Team Meetings

You may have rolled your eyes reading this chapter title. A lot of business owners dread team meetings. Honestly, I only started to love them when I realized they were multiplying my time! A one-hour meeting of my time can send a dozen people off working congruently on one vision. Perhaps you're thinking that since I've already introduced you to the Same Pager™ that you don't need to meet as often or at all. The answer is still yes. Your Same Pager™ is your road map, and in your meetings, you'll go into detail of what it takes to reach your goal and who is assigned to do what each step of the way.

You may still be thinking that meetings can be an unnecessary waste of time. I suggest you keep track of how many times you're interrupted throughout the day with questions. In fact, I want you to track exactly that for a week. Each time you're interrupted, document it. When I have clients do this, they're blown away. The amount of time they spend responding to texts, emails, project management software, and people physically knocking on their door really adds up. I'm certain it far exceeds any time they would have spent in a team meeting. A "quick question" that happens several times a day, multiplied by the number of people on your team, could be dramatically reduced with a quick, *effective* meeting. Give it a try and test it yourself.

Effective meetings not only reduce daily interruptions, they help support everyone on the team and enable them to achieve their own daily and weekly tasks, as well as keeping everyone focused on the goal. I meet some business owners who say, "I didn't get into business to sit in meetings all day." I get it. When you're passionate about who you serve and what you do, a meeting can feel like a waste of time. Effective meetings should only be about what you do and who you serve. When you do them correctly, you'll understand why they're so important.

Three Reasons

Don't get me wrong. Meetings absolutely can be a waste of time when there's no direction and they're inefficient. For example:
- 5 people @ $20/hr. = $100/meeting with weekly meetings costing $5,200/year.
- 5 people @ $30/hr. = $150/meeting with weekly meetings costing $7,800/year.
- 5 people @ $50/hr. = $250/meeting with weekly meetings costing $13,000/year.

They can be expensive and suck a lot of valuable revenue-generating time. Ten people in a one-hour meeting is ten hours lost every week for over 500 hours lost in a year.

To be effective, the three biggest reasons to hold a meeting are to determine:
1. Are our priorities in check to hit our goals?
2. Are we on track with our goals?

3. Does anyone need support achieving their specific goals and priorities?

If you hold a meeting to address those three things, you'll be in great shape. I'm assuming you're onboard for not wasting time and money, so here is the blueprint for an effective, successful meeting:
- The right people are in the room
- Meeting frequency
- Meeting length
- Leader
- Agenda
- Assigned accountability
- Get it on the calendar
- Location

Before we dive into each of these, first confirm that a meeting actually needs to take place. Presuming you have a project management software program, it's there for a reason. (If you don't, you need to research this!) Unless there is a discussion that's needed, you can make an announcement, issue directives, etc. through your project management software. If you determine a meeting is needed, let's look at the blueprint items individually.

The Right People: I'll tell you immediately that *you* don't need to be in every meeting. At some point, I realized this and I removed myself from two of the daily huddles, so I'd have two mornings/week to write. I had the most appointments on my calendar and needed some white space. However, I didn't skip the meetings until they were running smoothly and consistently. Additionally, you have to ensure that everyone in the meeting needs to be in the meeting. Otherwise, it is a waste of time and money. I've had people say, "Oh, I'd love to listen in on what's happening in marketing even though I'm in fulfillment." I used to let this happen because I thought it would be good for folks to know what was happening throughout the company. The result? I lost revenue-generating time from the departments that were not directly affected. Now we provide debriefs on weekly meetings from each department, and that's how everyone finds out what's going on in our various departments. We want to be transparent across the company. These debriefs are more cost-effective than paying everyone to sit in every meeting.

Determine who's really needed:
- Entire team (yes, sometimes)
- Leadership
- Department specific
- Program specific
- 1:1

Frequency: For each meeting, you need to determine whether it's a one-off (discuss a single issue) or if meeting about the topic needs to recur. If the latter, determine if that recurrence is weekly, monthly, quarterly, or annually, keeping in mind that as you progress, meeting frequency will likely change.

When we first created Well-Oiled Operations™ Mastery, we met weekly. We wanted prompt, if not immediate, feedback: What were clients saying? What were their results? Did we need to add, edit, or delete anything to make this great program even better? As we started to refine the program, we achieved what we set out to do and deliver the results we promised. Once that happened, we reduced the meeting frequency from weekly to quarterly to keep tabs on the program and clients' successes.

On the other hand, we've had some meetings that we believed would be one-offs, only to discover as the meeting progressed that there was more we needed to discuss, so we increased the frequency. Here's what I want you to remember about frequency: Allow time between meetings to actually implement the action steps that result from the meeting. Don't think that because you increase frequency, you'll achieve your goals or solve any problems faster. If meetings occur too frequently, what you'll likely hear in the next meeting is, "Yes, I'm still working on that." Allow time for implementation!

Meeting Length: So how long does an effective meeting need to last? The simplest answer is as long as it needs to. I've been guilty of having meetings that were too long or too short. If you schedule a meeting for two hours, you may find that it stretches to that length simply because it could, where in reality, half that time would have sufficed. If you schedule 30 minutes, you may find you're rushing at the 25-minute point without having accomplished anything. Get in the habit of sticking to your agenda, and when you're done, you're done. Don't waste extra time for small talk. Get started promptly, stay on track, and adjourn when you're done. No one, even your team members, want to waste time.

Meeting Leader: Just because you're the boss doesn't mean you have to lead every (or any) meeting. The point of any meeting is to move your business forward, and depending on the topic and meeting goal, someone else on your team may be the right person to lead the meeting, including deciding who should attend, frequency, length, and agenda.

In our company, our daily huddle (in which we determine what has to happen that day) is led by one of my team members, and our weekly meeting is led by another team member. Not only I am not the leader for either of these meetings, there are times I don't even attend due to my own travel schedule. I don't want my schedule to disrupt progress, and at this point, my team has become really great at leading meetings that run as smoothly as they would if I were there. In fact, I personally don't want to lead any meetings that I attend. I want to be there as a participant, fully focused on my zone of genius, which is being the visionary. If I'm leading the meeting and keeping track of the agenda and ensuring participants are staying on topic, I can't participate as much as I'd like.

Agenda: Like your road map for leading the company, the agenda is the road map for leading the meeting. You should have an agenda for every single meeting if you want them to truly be effective. Recurring meetings may have a standing agenda, but don't make that assumption. The meeting leader should review the agenda and make any needed updates prior to the meeting. Agendas will keep you on track and help you and your team prioritize the ideas and issues that result from the meeting. They also help minimize small talk and stay focused on having a productive meeting.

Assigned Accountability: Effective meetings create a lot of discussion. The worst thing that can happen is talking about a lot of issues without someone taking accountability and ownership for the topic and the follow-up or action step implementation. You never want to get to the next meeting and hear, "Oh, I thought he was doing that." A notetaker can be really helpful – someone who is catching ideas and tasks, assigning them, recapping, and letting everyone know who's accountable. Your notetaker should not be your meeting leader. They have enough to keep track of in running the meeting and sticking to the agenda. Ensure your meeting leader has someone else filling in when the notetaker happens to be absent. Putting it on paper paves the way to greater accountability.

> *Never leave a meeting without knowing who does what by when!*

Get it on the calendar: If you don't have a company-wide calendar, it's time to get one. There are plenty of calendar tools available or you can build one using a simple spreadsheet to which everyone has access, like Google Docs or similar. You don't want to schedule a meeting, only to find one of the key participants has a conflict and won't be there. We share via Google Calendar, so everyone knows when and where to be, and these dates are non-negotiable. Team members know they aren't allowed to take consults, coaching calls, or other appointments during our set times. They are that important!

Location: Love it or hate it, the pandemic put Zoom front and center as a meeting platform. We use it for 90 percent of our meetings. Even in our brick-and-mortar location, our weekly meetings are via Zoom. Remember when I said meetings should be only as long as needed? Sometimes, ours are very short – eight to ten minutes and we're done. It doesn't make sense to dedicate time to get to the meeting (even walking through the building), waiting for everyone to arrive with accompanying small talk, and then accomplish what needs to be done in nearly less time than assembling for the meeting. That time adds up. With Zoom, it's log on, meet, log off, and back to work.

While most of my team members for my consulting company live locally, most work remotely, so Zoom meetings absolutely make the most sense. However, our quarterly and annual meetings are held in person. They're always longer (justifying traveling to the meeting site), and it helps to build and maintain a personal connection between team members. Having in-person meetings once in a while is a must.

Getting Started

Having coached countless clients, I know that starting and running effective meetings is one of the hardest things to implement. It can feel daunting and is often one of those areas where you simply don't know where to start. You may have been a participant in plenty of ineffective meetings yourself and believe that no meeting is better than a bad one. We offer an entire meeting process inside the Well-Oiled Operations[TM] Mastery program.

Here's where I want you to start if you haven't been having meetings or haven't been having effective meetings. Determine what you should cover in a weekly meeting and create the agenda. These meetings do not need to happen on Mondays or Fridays; any day will work. Whichever day you choose, plan an hour to start. If you have a small team, you can include everyone. For larger teams, you may break these weekly meetings by departments. Remember: you do not need to be the meeting leader! The idea behind these meetings is to get everyone on the same page. Share your Same Pager[TM] and review and assign the tasks that need to be done that week as they relate to your goals and vision.

The next thing I coach my clients on regarding meetings are the 1:1 meetings. Once you start having team meetings, you'll quickly see who doesn't mind speaking up in front of the group and who remains quiet. That happens naturally, but you never want your quiet team members to be unclear of what's expected of them or to leave the meeting feeling either overwhelmed or frustrated. One of the biggest game changers for my dance and music school over a decade ago was incorporating 1:1s. Each full-time person gets weekly time with their manager. (Our part-timers get a monthly 1:1). This meeting does not have to be long. The idea behind it is a quick check-in and an opportunity for each one to speak up about what they need. (To see our 1:1 agenda, visit: www.welloiledoperations.com/bookbonuses.)

Once you start incorporating 1:1s, you should notice a big difference. You won't be wondering what everyone is working on, and your team will feel more supported than ever as well as really understand your vision and where you want the company to go. Remember as a kid asking a million times, "Are we there yet?" It's human nature to want to know where we're going and how long it's going to take. We might stop asking as adults, but we still want to know. Your team members will appreciate having this information on a weekly basis – here's where we want to go, here's where we are, here's how we think we can get there.

As you begin hosting these two types of meetings, keep your eyes open for the need for other meetings. You may realize you need to add department meetings or leadership team meetings. Once you (and everyone on your team) have positive experiences from effective meetings, you'll learn that they don't take up your time – they multiply it, and you'll be open to the idea of even more!

Creating Your Own Well-Oiled Operation

- Team meetings are a must, but ensure you are addressing the three reasons to have a meeting:
    1. Are our priorities in check to hit our goals?

2. Are we on track with our goals?
3. Does anyone need support achieving their specific goals and priorities?

- Keep the blueprint front and center when planning every and any meeting.
- Pick a consistent day/time for your weekly meeting and get it on the calendar.
- Decide if it will include leadership or everyone.
- Watch for other meetings that spark and add them to the calendar.

How would you score yourself right now on effective meetings?

- Red: No consistent meetings; you schedule them when you need them or you fail to accomplish anything through a meeting.
- Yellow: Some of this is in place but definitely still have some work to do.
- Green: You have consistent, effective meetings that are on the calendar with agendas that you stick to.

What needs to happen from this chapter? (Don't want to write in this book, download the workbook at www.welloiledoperations.com/bookbonuses)

Clean up: What can we remove?

_____
_____
_____
_____
_____

Tighten up: What can we speed up?

_____
_____
_____
_____
_____

Scale up: How can we plan for growth?

_____
_____
_____
_____
_____

Don't forget to snag our 1:1 agenda for free at: www.welloiledoperations.com/bookbonuses

Chapter Five:
Better Boundaries & Communication

When I started to create the Well-Oiled Operations™ Mastery program, I conducted about ten 1:1 VIP days with clients. I wanted to spend an entire day really understanding and grasping what their biggest challenges were. I came prepared for the day with an agenda of what I thought business owners would need. I thought my agenda was almost perfect, but I lacked the one thing every one of the VIP clients needed. They needed to learn how to create better boundaries and improve communication skills with their own clients and team members. A lot of them felt stuck. Stuck with bad clients who didn't respect their time and stuck with employees who interrupted them all day long. I'm sure many of them wanted me to agree that their clients and employees were over the top and demanding too much. However, in every case, I had to share the harsh truth, "You get what you tolerate. You set the tone at the beginning, and now they think this is how you do business." That's the bad news. The good news is that you can change their behavior by changing yours.

Now you're probably thinking about that and ready to tell me, "Oh, you don't know John. He doesn't like change." Or, "No, Stacy. Natasha really does have expectations that are too high." I've worked with enough clients to know that a lot of the bad behavior from clients, prospects, and team members was something that you tolerated, and perhaps you've tolerated it so long that you don't believe it can change. Even if someone's been a client for many years or an employee for a decade, trust me, I can help you.

I promise you this: you are never stuck. You have a choice to move forward. Let me say that again: You get to decide. The ***right*** people know that what you've been doing – tolerating – is more than necessary, and they won't be surprised by your price increase or your new communication requests. I'm not saying this will be easy. Notice I said, "the right people." Yes, some people will have a problem with it. In that case, you thank them for their time as a client or team member and wish them well.

At some point, we outgrow certain relationships, and you'd better believe that I've fired clients over the last 20 years. Let's not forget how and why it started: either you hired the wrong person or you've allowed the wrong client to pay you. Fail to recognize that, and you'll be making the same mistake over and over. You can't blame them if they lied in the interview or became crazy in their demands and expectations once they started paying you. Be honest. There have been red flags that you ignored… but that was the old you. Let's start fresh and put better boundaries in place.

Boundaries = Benefits

Adding boundaries has nothing but benefits. When you create better boundaries, you'll invite people to join you inside those boundaries, or if they ignore them, you invite them to leave and find someone else to take advantage of – not you. Chalk it up as a win.

As a business owner, I know you want more time, so we have to start there. I assure you that when you set up your preferred method of communication and the frequency of how often you'll check that communication, it will transform your life. Get too many emails or texts? Very simply, the more you check emails, the more emails you'll get. The more you check your phone and reply to texts, the more texts you'll get. We are going to massively condense the communication you receive by not only putting boundaries in place but also by making you a better communicator.

If you're someone who checks that email when it dings or every time you see that little red dot on your phone indicating a text, you've conditioned people to expect that you're going to answer quickly and effective replies are out the window. Here's an example (and I'm sure you've experienced this):

Person A: "Hey I'd love to set up a time to meet, let me know when you're free."

Person B: "Okay, cool. Let's do it, I'm free Monday and Tuesday"

Person A: "Shoot, Monday and Tuesday are the only days that don't work for me."

Person B: "What about Wednesday?"

Person A: "I could do Wednesday afternoon!"

Person B: "No, unfortunately not, what does next week look like?"

And then this goes on and on. Don't play a part in bad communication.

Once you set a limit on checking email to once or twice a day, max, and let people know that, they will become more concise, or else that communication string I just used as an example will take days to play out. The simple act of reducing the number of times you check email will make those people communicating with you be more efficient. You'll change your behavior (fewer checks), so as a result, they'll change their behavior (better communication). Let's look at that example again and see how it can be better:

Person A: "Hey I'd love to set up a time to meet, let me know when you're free."

If this is a "yes" for Person B: "Great here's my calendar link. My schedule is pretty tight, so what you see is really my only open availability. If those times don't work, just wait a little bit because each week more availability opens up."

If this is a "not yet" for Person B: "I wish I could. I have a few massive projects on my plate right now and my schedule is jam packed. Reach back in _____ and let's see if we can schedule something."

If this is a "no" for Person B: "Thanks for thinking of me! I wish I had the time, but right now my focus is on _____. I've dedicated all of my extra time to complete this. <Then insert your favorite closing> Wish you well, best of luck, take care!"

Here's what I want you to see: Just because someone wants to meet does not mean you are obligated to agree. Set a boundary.

A calendar link is a must! If you tell me your assistant does all of your scheduling, it's still a must, or you're wasting their time playing a part in the first example of trying to set a meeting. A calendar link also helps you set a boundary and establish when you're free without someone trying to squeeze into your day when you don't want to schedule something.

My appointments are all on Thursdays each week. When I share my calendar link, the recipient only sees Thursday slots. In fact, they'll only see Thursday afternoon slots as I save the mornings for urgent things that pop up at the last minute. I also only book myself out three weeks in advance, and each week my calendar opens the subsequent week, which is why I tell people that if they can't find an opening, wait a week as more slots will open. It is very clear that this is my availability and deters people from asking for a different time.

Do I ever deviate from this? Yes… if I'm interested and deviating is the only way to find a mutual accommodation. For example, when I interview some pretty big names on my podcast, like Suze Orman or a *New York Times* best-selling author, they may only provide two dates or times… period. They're actually setting their own boundary with a take-it-or-leave-it approach. If I want to take it, I'll rearrange my schedule, but those instances are rare. I find too many clients rearrange their schedules for things they don't want to attend or find valuable. That behavior has to stop and stop now.

Another thing I want you pay attention to: Did you notice how I (Person B) ended the email when I knew I was a "no"? The last sentence can get people into trouble. If you don't have any interest, never suggest "reach back later" or something that's equally open-ended. You know what happens if you do? They reach back later, and now you're in an unnecessary email dance again. Don't play this game because you'll lose every time. Be honest. If it's a no, let them know that. It's better for both of you. No one wants to be led on.

The Cost of Bad Boundaries

With bad (or worse, no) boundaries, you don't just lose time. You'll also lose money. It could be overspending on payroll for an employee not getting the job done or a client not paying for all the extras you keep throwing in without adjusting the invoice. You may think you're over-delivering, but there is a point at which they're taking advantage of you. Let me be clear: you're both allowing it.

I was recently coaching a client who's in a high-paying profession, probably one of the highest in hourly rates. Her own clientele are highly paid professionals. In looking at her numbers, overall, her monthly retainers looked great – a few thousand per client. However, when I looked at the hours she was putting in, she was actually making less than minimum wage. She's serving people making hundreds of dollars/hour doing work they aren't smart enough to do, which is why they hired her, and she wasn't charging nearly enough. She'd be better off working at Starbucks.

I had to dole out some tough love to her that day because no amount of money is worth running yourself into the ground. Your health will be affected; your family will be affected; every aspect of your life will be affected. Don't chase money that way. You'll never be happy. Her real problem was that she promised an outcome and quoted a price. She didn't realize it would take her 25 hours, but she felt she had to honor her quote. Ever been there?

So what do you do when you provide a quote and realize you've underestimated the time needed? Here's what I would do: I would finish the project as promised. A bad estimate is your fault, and no one appreciates their vendor quoting one thing and then changing it once they've started. It's bad business and a surefire way to lose a repeat client. So you bite the bullet and complete the project. Upon delivery (and here's the important part), you say, "I want you to know that I didn't realize how long this would take, and that was my fault. However, moving forward, if you would like me to continue working with you, here's what the rate will be."

You give them the choice to continue or not. That's fair. Unfortunately, I've worked with plenty of clients who felt they were locked into the worst rates forever. No, just give your clients a fair heads-up regarding the new rates and the time frame at which they'll be effective. In the case of my client's situation, she was genuinely nice and wanted to be helpful, so she kept throwing in bonuses at no additional charge. Do that, and you will begin to become resentful thinking, "This isn't fair; they aren't even paying me for this." Well, it's on you.

Escaping the Chaos

So, if you're reading this and seeing that you're guilty of not setting boundaries and it's landed you in a mess and is contributing to unnecessary chaos, how do you get out of it. I have your answer in three steps.

Step one: Assess where you are lacking boundaries or have bad ones. When does it happen and with whom? Write down the names of the problem people. Let's be honest, it's not all of your clients; neither is it all of your team members. There are certain people who will take whatever you give (and then some), so it feels like a much heavier burden than with others.

Step two: With your list of names, determine what you would like the relationship with each person to look like. What is fair? What was the original agreement and how far have you allowed it to get off track?

Step three: Write down how you'll handle things from this point forward. Depending on the person, it might be an email, text, or phone call. Maybe it's a change in policy for a group of clients or team members. In some cases, a group communication may be best, so it doesn't seem like you're calling a particular individual out. Remember to take ownership; it's on you. Blame yourself, not them.

By resetting the tone, you let them know how things are changing. If people expect you to check your email constantly and they are used to and expecting a prompt or even an immediate response, activate an autoresponder: "Thanks for your email. To improve my productivity, I am now only checking email once/day between 3:00-4:00 p.m. CST and will reply/respond at my earliest convenience." I would also send this as a message to those people who may need to know in advance. Once your autoresponder has been in place for a few weeks, you can remove it if you'd like because you've now re-set the expectation.

> *When you change your own behavior, you magically change theirs as well.*

We want to train people that email is never urgent. If it's a customer service inbox, you'll need to figure out how promptly you want someone to reply. It doesn't have to be you. In my business, we check the customer service inbox three times/daily – once at the start of the shift, once in the middle, and once before we wrap up the day. With that schedule, emails are being answered within a few hours, except for those that come in overnight. At the very least, we reply within one business day, and that is entirely acceptable. My team also appreciates this schedule and not being inundated with dings and interruptions. I want them to be strategically opening emails and getting the inbox to zero without being at someone's beck and call, becoming far less efficient and productive themselves.

This approach can be done with any device. You don't have to answer your phone just because it rings. In fact, mine rarely rings because I've set it to silent for any unknown callers. I only hear a ring if one of my contacts is calling. You can set your outbound message to mirror your autoresponder: "Thanks for calling. I check voice mail at <insert your parameters> and will return your call at that time."

Some of these changes will take a bit of time, both for you and others to adjust to. You have to be okay with that. If you've been allowing this to happen for months, years, and maybe even decades, it's going to take time to create the new habit.

Team Member Communication

Setting boundaries with clients may seem like the bigger challenge because they are, after all, paying you. While you can have the same expectation of team members because you're paying them, the number of team members reaching out to you can be the challenge. Remember my client, Kristina from Chapter 1? She had 30 team members contacting her with "just a quick question." Once we revamped her organizational chart, she went from 30 to only five. You don't need everyone on your team to have direct access to you all the time. You can even limit contact with a small team. All you have to do is put a gatekeeper in front of you. Instead of allowing anyone to call, text, or email you, let them know the best way to get support and answers to their questions.

You have to decide:

- Your preferred method of communication.
- When you're going to check email, attend team meetings, and reply to notifications via a project management software program.
- Which project management software you want to use if you haven't already implemented one.
- How often you expect team members to check notifications and the expected response time.

    This is where an organizational chart is a must. It tells everyone who reports to whom, who they can reach out to directly, and who they can't. Only my direct reports reach out to me directly. If a team member has something to communicate, they tell their manager and it goes up the line. You might think that slows down productivity and innovation; however, the things people think I need to know can already be handled by their manager. Most of the requests or suggestions never cross my desk (my managers are handling them), so it frees my time to work on the things only I can do in my business.

    If you notice balls are being dropped, deadlines missed, and customer mistakes occurring, that indicates a lack of communication and/or ownership. Again, your organizational chart should be clarifying who does what and who is responsible to see that it gets done. Be crystal clear and set expectations.

When I coach clients about setting boundaries, they get excited to implement them because they see all the benefits. Then I'll get a message from them: "I set the boundary, but I am still getting texts." Or "I told him John is his manager, but he still comes to me." Remember when you were a child? You knew exactly when your parents meant business or when you could continue to ask, hoping they'd give in. Nothing's changed. This is how boundaries, especially new ones, work. Whether someone is testing you, doesn't care about this new system, thinks it's stupid, or simply forgets, you have to be the stern parent who doesn't *allow* it. When I first started, my phone number was public knowledge to all employees. Although they knew they were supposed to contact their manager if they were sick, they'd sometimes shoot me a text, hoping I'd help them out. When I caved and did help them, they continued to do it. It was my own fault. I finally decided that I'd had enough and knew I could no longer allow it. So my reply to a text about an employee reporting out sick: "Sorry to hear you're not feeling well. Make sure to reach out to your manager, so we can cover your absence." Guess how many more times that person reached out to me? None. Why? They learned my boundary and knew they were wasting their time.

Yes, sometimes you are going to have team members who repeatedly try again and again. Repeat your message and stick to your guns. When they realize you are not the solution (or the shortcut), they'll learn. You may think that it's easier to provide the answer to that "quick question," but you're only continuing to break your own boundary by doing so. It's just like parenting.

Another business owner I know had also given out her phone number to all her employees and was getting bogged down in interruptions and not getting anything done. So she changed the rule and told her employees they could only call her in an emergency. When her phone rang and the contact was an employee, she'd answer, "Hello so-and-so, what's your emergency?" Of course, almost all the time they'd say, "Well, it's not technically an emergency..." to which she'd reply, "Great, then save it for the next time we meet." People stopped calling with non-emergencies pretty quickly!

A lack of boundaries is one of the biggest problems I see with my clients, and I could go on and on. I want to wrap up this topic by telling you that you must take the drama out of communications by using facts, not feelings. I do not allow vague thoughts or feelings to be shared. These are things I never want to hear:

- Ads aren't going well.
- Sales are down.
- Everyone is complaining about it.

Nope. Those don't work for me. It tells me nothing. Give me facts. I want to know what you spent on ads today and what we made. Which product sales were down (to the penny) for the last seven days? Who complained and how many complaints did we get? I set the expectation, and my team knows that vague statements just won't fly with me. I suggest you do the same. When someone issues a vague statement, stop them and ask for specifics. If they can't provide specifics, tell them to find out what they are and then return. Communication should always focus on the facts, not feelings, between you and your team members and between one team member and another.

Without a doubt, a lack of boundaries is costing you. No more saying "yes" unless the request lights you up. Focus on the activities that directly relate to your Same Pager™ to achieve your goals. If you keep your actions and boundaries where they are now, your outcomes are going to stay the same as well. You need to become the next level CEO who sets boundaries or be satisfied to stay right where you are... next year and the year after that. Is that really what you want? I didn't think so.

Creating Your Own Well-Oiled Operation

- Assess where are you allowing bad (or no) boundaries to happen and with whom.
- List everyone with whom you have a boundary issue and decide what you want this relationship to look like.
- Send out an email, text, or call and re-set the tone.
- Set an autoresponder or outgoing voice mail explaining when anyone can expect you to retrieve the message and respond.

- Remind the team of the org chart and who they should be contacting.
- Pick a project management software program if you haven't already!

How would you score yourself right now on boundaries and communication?
- Red: I am constantly interrupted all day from clients or team members.
- Yellow: Some of this is in place but definitely still have some work to do.
- Green: I have excellent boundaries and people respect them.

What needs to happen from this chapter? (Don't want to write in this book, download the workbook at www.welloiledoperations.com/bookbonuses)

Clean up: What can we remove?
_____
_____
_____
_____
_____

Tighten up: What can we speed up?
_____
_____
_____

_____
_____

Scale up: How can we plan for growth?

_____
_____
_____
_____

If you want some of my scripts for better boundaries and saying no, go to:

www.welloiledoperations.com/bookbonuses

Chapter Six:
Solid Foundations

I'm sure I don't have to tell you the importance of having a solid foundation. If you want your business to run smoothly, much of that depends on your team. The most important time for any new hire (both for you and the person you hired) is the first 90 days after joining the team. That time sets the tone for everything else that will follow.

The reason it's also critical for you has everything to do with the boundaries you set, the importance of which we just covered. If you're lax in what you tolerate at the start, it will be much harder to correct down the road. Make sure you explain your boundaries clearly and from the start. This also helps set up your new hire for success because you've provided expectations about what success looks like for your team members.

Many of the business owners I've coached have not properly onboarded their new hires. They didn't explain company values, review the employee handbook, or cover what is expected. Maybe you're also guilty of this. There are things in your head that you've assumed your team knows. Or you think much of this is common sense, yet without having it explained, your new hire (or existing team) may never think to do it. I can tell you right now what everyone on your team lacks – the ability to read your mind. Relying on mind reading is never the right business strategy, yet so many business owners expect it every day and then place the blame on their team when things go awry.

If you find yourself in this position, let me share some good news: It's never too late to properly onboard a team member, even if they've been with you for ten years. You want everyone to be onboard and moving in the same direction, and this is not as big a project as it sounds. Much of it can be done in a group meeting, with just a few things needing to be done one-on-one.

To start, I suggest holding a company meeting (in person or virtual) and simply explain that you lacked a solid onboarding process when you hired them and that you're now creating one for all new hires moving forward. To ensure everyone is on the same page, you're sharing everything new hires will hear. It's a great idea to record this, so you create a library of videos to share with new hires later. It can save you time in the future, and these videos can be invaluable when you hire remote team members.

Many business owners feel they don't have time to hire, and even worse, they don't have time to train. Creating a video library will expedite this process. Your new hire can begin consuming this information without it taking up your time initially. You can then have a 1:1 meeting with them to answer questions. This library can be created inside your project management software, as an online course, or hidden in your website on pages that are password-protected.

One of our rockstar clients, Carina Gardner, founder of Design Suite, shared that after implementing this strategy, she went from spending ten hours onboarding a new hire to one hour. She's saving nine hours of training time for every team member she brings on, and she's been onboarding about two new team members every month. That time really adds up!

You may not be hiring that frequently or you may not be spending ten hours on new hire training; however, I'm sure you still feel pressed for time, and a lack of time means you are rushing through the training process. I know when that happens, things like how the company got started and what the company values are and how they apply get pushed aside and usually never covered. Those might be the most important things you share! When you have recorded new hire training, you've solved that problem.

If you haven't had a formal onboarding process, you'll also want to share certain paperwork that needs to be signed if this has never been done (and be sure to do this moving forward). This includes things like:

- Job offer
- Non-disclosure agreements
- Employee handbook
- Social media policy
- Non-compete agreements

If an existing employee or a new hire refuses to sign, use that as a red flag. Ask what they're opposed to and why. I caution you: do not let this slide. For example, if someone suggests they're not interested in a non-compete, do not excuse them from signing. I had someone who wouldn't sign, and when I pressed for the reason, she said she "had to keep her options open." As in: option to become my competitor. I train her for weeks and share everything that's made me successful and then she uses that for herself? No way. We had to part ways.

Your solid foundation is all about getting a team member:

- On the same page by understanding their job description and how it contributes to and plays a part in the company's big picture.
- Clear on their key performance indicators and how they'll be tracked and measured.
- Organized with a plan for progress from day one.
- Excited, motivated, and with an understanding of what it looks like to win.

Reading this, you may realize that you've never given proper attention to this. Again, it's never too late to onboard even your existing team members. I once had someone who was never properly onboarded, and when I discovered it, we were already a year into her employment. I explained it was a disservice and would like to properly onboard her in this position. She was grateful that I gave her the extra time. With existing or new employees, proper onboarding can eliminate or certainly reduce future discipline issues. Once you've properly onboarded, if it's still not working out, it becomes clear to both parties that it's time for you to let them go. If there's a disciplinary issue, you've already clarified what the steps are (e.g., verbal warning, written warning, etc.) that you'll take prior to finally terminating.

Onboarding Process

When we onboard a new team member, we do a daily check-in during the first 30 days. We also do a daily check-in for 30 days after someone is promoted to a new position. These daily check-ins keep everyone on track, and in 30 days, you'll have much greater clarity about having a rockstar team member or someone who's a mismatch and should be let go.

Our new hires create an end-of-day report with three simple questions answered:
1. Where did you win?
2. Where did you struggle?
3. What are your priorities for tomorrow?

The next morning, they review their answers with their immediate manager. Their manager can acknowledge their wins, train on their struggles, and help them prioritize for the day. This meeting can be as short as ten minutes or as long as 30 minutes. Some business owners that I coach think this is a lot of support, but if it's a longer meeting, that clearly indicates more training is needed. I assure you, pretty soon, the daily review of those end-of-day reports will show fewer struggles, more wins, and better prioritization.

Around the 30-day mark, we reduce these check-ins to about three times a week, and reduce again at the 60-day mark. By the time we get to 90 days, it's once a week. When you provide this level of attention and support, you'll start to see a drastic difference in how fast your team member is on their way to making a difference for your company. This time frame and the check-ins provide better clarity in the quality of the new hire and how well they are aligning with your organization.

Review their job description every 30 days. It gives your new hire a chance to point out if they haven't been trained on something that you envision they'll do. The goal with great onboarding practices is to get rid of any wrong fits before you get to the 90-day mark. It is simply too costly to keep them. If there's any doubt, err on the side of letting them go. Let's be honest. They aren't going to work harder or try harder after their first 90 days. If they can't perform what you need them to do, that's a sign of a bad fit.

A good onboarding process is more than just talking. Yes, at the beginning, they may be watching your videos where you're talking and explaining. It's important to demonstrate more than talk – it's also a time to show and practice.

In our studios, we teach assistants how to greet students and parents. If we bring in a new coach for Well-Oiled Operations™ Mastery, we have them shadow and observe call after call before we send them out on their own. Imagine their greater level of confidence when they've seen it in action over and over!

Unfortunately, many business owners throw new hires into their roles and expect them to know what they're doing. Again, I know for a fact you don't have anyone on your team who's a mind reader! They'll either work on projects that aren't a top priority because they don't know the priority or they'll focus on what they do know that may not be as important.

Once you solidify your new hire process by going through it with your existing team members, onboarding your next new hire will be a breeze. It will be easier for you, but every bit as important – you'll be making a good first impression. That first impression can make or break whether someone goes all-in for you, chooses to stay at all, or immediately begins looking for a better fit somewhere else.

When I interviewed Joey Coleman, author of *Never Lose a Customer Again: Turn Any Sale into Lifelong Loyalty in 100 Days* on the *Well-Oiled Operations*™ podcast, he mentioned what he calls "hire's remorse" and likened it to buyer's remorse in which a consumer second guesses their decision. New hires can do the same thing. We don't want them second guessing their decision to take the job or wonder if they are a good fit for the position. When they join your team, you want them to understand what winning looks like, hear your company story and values, vision, and mission, so they will be wowed by the opportunity in front of them. Most small business owners don't do this.

How much money is wasted on team member inefficiencies because no one has taken the time to teach them? How many hours are wasted by new hires working on mindless activities trying to look busy? You will never have a well-oiled business if you don't fix these problems now. In fact, things are guaranteed to get messier as you attempt to scale your business.

Creating Your Own Well-Oiled Operation

- Onboard all of your current team members if you have not had a solid process in place to which you've *consistently* adhered.
- Record these sessions to begin building a library for new hires.
- Create proper documents and contracts and have everyone on your team sign them. A refusal to sign is a red flag.
- Conduct daily check-ins with new hires, having them answer the three simple questions:
    1. Where did you win?
    2. Where did you struggle?
    3. What are your priorities for tomorrow?
- It's not all talk. Demonstrate and role play as needed.

How would you score yourself right now on having a solid foundation?
- Red: No onboarding systems, expectations have not been clearly set, lack of training in onboarding and/or after 90 days.

- Yellow: Some of this is in place but definitely still have some work to do.
- Green: We have a rock solid onboarding system.

What needs to happen from this chapter? (Don't want to write in this book, download the workbook at www.welloiledoperations.com/bookbonuses)

Clean up: What can we remove?
_____
_____
_____
_____

Tighten up: What can we speed up?
_____
_____
_____
_____

Scale up: How can we plan for growth?
_____
_____
_____
_____

We offer a free quiz to help you figure out how you rank and determine what you should be working on next. If you haven't discovered your Scale Score yet, go to www.welloiledoperations.com/bookbonuses

Chapter Seven:
Hiring & Firing

When I started my dance studio business over 20 years ago, I quickly found myself in over my head when it came to managing daily operations. I was definitely the CEO – Chief **Everything** Officer. I already shared how I took a call and updated a customer's credit card information... in my wedding dress. I will never forget how much the business was running me, rather than the other way around. And I was not alone. Even the most seasoned, established entrepreneurs, like those attending conferences designed for seven-figure businesses, have trouble leaving work at work. It is actually so commonplace that it serves as validation to everybody else: "This is normal; this is okay." Just because it seems normal and everyone is doing it, doesn't mean it has to be your normal.

When I became overwhelmed, overworked, and underpaid, I decided this wasn't going to be *my* normal. Although I started as a one-woman show, today, I have over 50 employees between my two businesses and dozens of contractors, too. I know entrepreneurs get nervous about hiring because they've heard having employees can be a nightmare, or perhaps they've already tried it and failed. They may be anxious about paying someone other than themselves. Those are valid points, but as someone who's been a solopreneur and someone who has several employees, I would never go back to being on my own without a team. Recently, I was gone for a week and a half but was never interrupted once. It was wonderful. The business kept running and revenue kept flowing in. Building a team is only a nightmare if you don't know who to hire, how to set boundaries, and how to lead. Fortunately, I'm going to share that with you right now.

Most entrepreneurs launch their businesses to create freedom, and freedom is getting to choose the things you want to do. When you implement the strategies I'm about to share, you'll see that you can learn to lead a team that allows everyone involved more freedom.

Steps to Take

Clarity always brings confidence. The more crystal clear about exactly why you want to hire someone and what their role in your company will look like, the more confidence you'll have bringing them onboard and setting them up for success. To start:

- Do a brain dump of all the tasks that need to be delegated.
- Get completely clear on the daily and weekly tasks for this new hire.
- Define what winning looks like long-term for this role you are creating.

There is a specific order to hiring, and when you get it wrong, it leads to letting people go, which is never fun. While there is a specific order, it is not cookie cutter. Let's examine, based on your role, the next position for which to hire and then where do you go from there.

Breaking it down, there are three main roles in every organization no matter the business or industry. When you're getting started, you fill all three. You may not be doing them well, but you're still in charge of handling them. They are:

- Product mastery: Customer fulfillment and retention.
- Marketing: Copywriting, graphics, social media, etc.
- Operations: Business management, systems setup, and maintenance.

Every business needs all three of these components in order to have long-term success. The question to ask is: "Who are you being naturally?" Do you love marketing? Gravitate toward systems and operations? Maybe you obsess over the product or service. I want you to rank yourself in these three areas with one being your zone of genius and three being your least favorite. Now, you may be good at all of them because, after all, you've gotten your business up and running; however, that doesn't mean you should keep all of them on your plate. If you have difficulty narrowing it down, keep the top two that most reflect your true zone of genius (and enjoyment) and delegate the third one.

Plan to hire for that third one to start. Once you've made that hire and your employee or contractor is up and running and generating revenue for the business, consider delegating the second. Then rinse and repeat: Once the person is up and running and getting a return, hire out for the last one. Before you stop me and say, "But that's what I enjoy most," I want you to remember that your role now becomes one of visionary. For example, although marketing is my own zone of genius, I don't want to "own" this department or balls will surely drop. I am definitely the visionary sharing my ideas and creating content, but someone else is in charge of the nuts and bolts – ensuring podcasts go out on time, posting on YouTube, and confirming that our social media posts are scheduled for two weeks in advance. I have provided the vision and instruction for each of these component areas and have hired people to see it through. At some point, you have to let go of being the "doer" in your organization.

If you're worried about the affordability of making a hire, remember, start small. You can hire part-time or on a contracted basis. You can start by getting an assistant for that third area and have them grow into the role before bringing them on as an employee. If you implement the strategies I'm teaching you, your team member will generate revenue – enough to cover their salary plus additional profit. It goes right back to clarity: define the role and how that role will boost revenue. Even if it is getting tasks off your plate (and not directly generating revenue), that is ultimately freeing you up for more revenue-generating activities. It's never a matter of *you* affording it; ask how the *business* can afford it.

Hiring Mistakes

I've hired a lot of people over the last 20 years, and yes, I've made a lot of mistakes. It wasn't easy in the beginning, and I want to share what I learned, so you can avoid making the same mistakes and achieve success faster.

Don't ignore your gut feeling. If there are red flags – late for the interview, reference check seemed "off," something said in the interview that made you cringe a bit – listen to your gut. Whenever I've ignored my gut feeling about someone, it has always led to termination down the road because those red flags kept getting bigger.

Don't hire someone similar to you. You actually want to find someone who's a bit opposite. What you don't see, you want them to. For example, you may be great at creative design but not great at catching typos. Your hire should complement you and be good at the things where you're weak. More of you is not what you need. Unfortunately, we like people who are like us, and that bias tends to carry right over to hiring. Business owners end up with a team that looks just like them. The result is that the owner's weakness is still the company's weakness. Hire for your weaknesses, so your business gets stronger. I'd love for you to listen to an incredible conversation I had on the topic "Diversity Advantages in the Marketplace" that I had with diversity, equity, and inclusion expert, Rhonda Moret. (Visit www.welloiledoperations.com/bookbonuses to hear it.)

Don't rely on a single recruiting source. Cast a wide net to catch your next hire. Don't forget social media and your email list. You never know if your client has a sister-in-law who may be perfect for that role. Some business owners fear that looks bad, but customers and prospects trust a company that's growing. Ask employees for recommendations, especially your rockstars. They probably hang out with people who have similar work ethics, team attitudes, etc. Referral bonuses for employees is another great way to hire quality people.

Don't wait too long. Desperate people hire desperate people. You don't want to be in the energy of "we'll take the next warm body" because you feel you need to fill a vacancy now. That is never sustainable and leads to expensive turnover and employees who cost you time and money. If you feel you'll be ready to fill the position in a month or two, it's better to hire now.

Don't hire alone. You can be easily convinced about a potential employee because their qualifications look great on paper. This perspective can lead you to miss red flags during the interview. A second opinion is critical. Bring in another team member, a manager, or even a spouse or friend if you don't have many team members yet. It's very helpful to have someone else listening during the interview process. If you're doing a virtual interview (and most of them start that way now), record it and have someone else watch it. If someone else is with you live, you don't have to go into a lot of detail about their role. For recordings, simply let them know you are recording it (and Zoom notifies all participants as well).

Don't move too quickly. You always want multiple rounds of interviews – at least two. Even if you absolutely love the person you're interviewing, subsequent rounds will allow you to see their consistency and if something pops up that did not during the first interview. You can ask the same questions in a different way. You'll discover very quickly who's showing up authentically and who's contradicting themselves.

Don't pay too much in the probationary period. We always enter a 90-day probationary period before someone officially joins the team. This is when we can see if they're as good as they seemed in the interview. New team members take time to get up and running and contributing to the revenue and bottom line. You can offer a lower rate during this period with an automatic raise at the 90-day mark. We're upfront and transparent about this approach during the interview and determine it on a case-by-case basis, depending on the level of expertise the new hire brings to the table.

Don't simply pay them what they've asked. You must know the going rate for the specific role in your industry. A candidate may pitch you a higher number, assuming you'll negotiate. Set the pay scale before you even meet the first candidate! When the discussion of compensation comes up, you'll know if it will be a good fit and if you're close.

Don't hire if you don't have time to train. Be clear about how and when you're going to train – how much time will be needed and what time can you give them. Block that time on your calendar. It might take a few months to get them up to speed, so go ahead and reserve that time now.

Hiring Best Practices

I just covered a lot of "don'ts," so now let's look at what you should do.

If you've used any of the job posting sites, you may have noticed that you get dozens of resumes within minutes (or even seconds) of posting. Sites and candidates can automate resume delivery when certain positions match their skills and keywords. It's possible that people who never laid eyes on your post are now applying for the position, and you certainly don't have time to weed through these dozens of potentially unqualified and uninterested candidates.

Instead, here's a strategy to find the cream of the crop with far less wasted time on your part, narrowing down the pool to the very best people: set it up so that the candidate does the work. You only want to review resumes of those who've taken the time to become familiar with your business and the position for which you're hiring. The reply email you use should be a generic inbox for which you set up an autoresponder email that invites them to take the next step. The next step can be an application or additional form to complete if they've already filled out an application. If they're not willing to take the extra steps, they've already saved you time. You can automatically go from dozens or hundreds of applications to a manageable handful.

Once you review the handful, you can then decide who you actually want to interview. The more you ask them to jump through hoops, the more people will fall off. You may be thinking that you want as many applicants as possible. Honestly, you don't. You want applicants who will be willing to do the work, and asking for extra steps showcases who these people are. You can invite candidates to submit a short video or introductory paragraph outlining why they feel they're the best fit. You can also provide a number for them to call and leave a voice mail explaining why they're excited about the opportunity and how they think they'll fit in with your organization.

Those who take these steps and put in the extra effort are the ones you'll actually want to hire! Once I'm down to two or three applicants, I always offer a sample ***paid*** project to complete as the last step of the hiring process. People who are committed and see themselves as the right fit will put in the work to complete this. Even if they already have a full-time job but are looking for a change, they will make time for the assignment. By comparing the work, you'll quickly see which of the final candidates is the winner. End by having the applicant sign the job offer and begin to onboard!

Parting Ways

As much as you'll refine your own hiring process as you go, inevitably, you'll bring someone on to your team who you shouldn't have. Learn from your mistake and let this person go as fast as humanly – and legally – possible. I know from consulting across the country and around the world that every state or country has its own employment laws. Consult with an attorney who knows the laws before terminating anyone, or it can cost you. When you stick to what we've covered (making them jump through hoops during the interview, reviewing their paid sample project, paying attention during the 90-day probationary period, and open and honest communication), your hire will stay longer and be a good team player, making terminations far less frequent.

However, you may not have known those strategies to this point in your business, and you have people on your team now who really shouldn't be there. First, ask yourself if you've done everything you can do to set this person up for success. You can't label them as "not good" if your own leadership has been sub-par or even non-existent. I can't tell you how many clients have joined Well-Oiled Operations™ Mastery, assuming they'll be letting someone go only to tell me in a month how much this employee has dramatically improved. If someone bought you a flower and you did nothing but look at it every day and it started to wilt, would you blame the flower? Of course not. You know you need to water it and place it in an environment in which it will thrive. Think about the wilting team member who you think has to go. Have you been watering them? Have you placed them in the sun or in a dark closet?

Obviously, not all of your underperforming team members are your fault. Honestly, there are some that no matter what I tell you or what you try, they'll never fit. For them, start by having an honest conversation. "Here is what I expect from this role. Do you want this? Does this work light you up? Is this still a good fit for you?" I'm very honest and let people know it's okay to say no. We want someone who loves the ride, and they won't hurt my feelings if that time, for whatever reason, has come to an end. I've noticed some people think they're doing you a favor by sticking around. I even had a client tell me that after having this conversation, the team member said, "No, it doesn't light me up, but I didn't want to leave after all you've done for me." Sometimes, they put off the difficult conversation. A simple conversation can end with the mutual agreement to part ways.

While I appreciate when it ends that way, that's not always how it goes. Some people will insist that they love what they're doing and believe they're doing great in their role. This is when you need to institute a 30-day performance review or Performance Improvement Plan. Re-set the expectations and be very clear about what you want to see over the next month. Meet weekly to review whether improvements are occurring. It will become very clear when the employee is missing the mark. We've had some team members see for themselves at the two-week mark that it isn't for them. Others go through the 30 days and either make improvements or understand why they're being terminated.

I've seen people make the needed improvements in the 30-day period; however, I know that I (or their manager) have to continue monitoring or they slip back into old, bad habits. When that happens, you need open, honest feedback. "I see it's only been another week and your performance is dropping again." This is the time to assess if they are truly capable of doing the job. If not, it's time for them to go. If so, it's probably that they don't want it enough, so also time to go. No one likes to terminate anyone. "He's a nice guy." Or "She's trying really hard." An underperformer (for whatever reason) doesn't just hurt the business – it's actually stealing from the business, from you, your team, and your team's families. The impact is often farther reaching than you image. The opportunity cost of not terminating is too large. I've never once worked with a client who regretted a termination. Instead, it usually brings relief. Your gut is telling you to fire them for a reason.

Hiring and firing are like any other skill set and one you must get good at. The people you bring on to your team will drastically change the top line and bottom line of your business. They can either make you excited to come to work or dread it. High performers want to work with other high performers. Keep your A-players and either coach up your Bs and Cs or let them go. Retaining underperformers brings down the whole team. Take your emotions out of it and determine who's contributing and who's not.

Creating Your Own Well-Oiled Operation

- Determine the position (product, marketing, or operations) for which you need to hire by assessing which one is furthest from your zone of genius, and that should be your first hire.
- Get very clear about the tasks involved for the new role and define what success looks like.
- Don't hire more of you. A diverse team is incredibly important.
- Review the most common hiring mistakes and take steps to avoid them.
- Make people jump through hoops to weed out unqualified candidates.
- Have your top two candidates complete paid sample projects before giving an offer.
- Find a professional in your state/country that can give you legal advice about firing.
- Don't delay having hard conversations with people who are underperforming.
- Start Performance Improvement Plans if necessary.

How would you score yourself right now on hiring and firing?
- Red: We've got Bs and Cs on the team who are currently underperforming.
- Yellow: Some of this is in place but definitely still have some work to do.

- Green: Everyone on our team is an A-player right now. We hire slow and fire fast.

What needs to happen from this chapter? (Don't want to write in this book, download the workbook at www.welloiledoperations.com/bookbonuses)

Clean up: What can we remove?

_____
_____
_____
_____
_____

Tighten up: What can we speed up?

_____
_____
_____
_____
_____

Scale up: How can we plan for growth?

_____
_____
_____
_____
_____

Listen to a bonus training with DEI expert, Rhoda Moret: Diversity Advantages in the Workplace: www.welloiledoperations.com/bookbonuses

Hiring & Firing

Phase 3

Well-Oiled Systems

Hiring & Firing

Chapter Eight:
SOPs

If you want to be well-oiled, you must have SOPs – standard operating procedures, or a.k.a. "systems." If you do everything else in this book but fail to have systems, you will always struggle. When I say "systems," I mean instructions that are carried out by your organization the same way every time. I know that systems get a bad rap, and some entrepreneurs are really negative about them, but I promise you: the people who have systems are not the ones complaining about them. The complainers are the ones who either don't have them or don't stick to them. Their complaints are really about struggling, and they're struggling because they don't believe in or have systems.

I can tell very quickly if a business has systems in place because it always comes down to consistent delivery of either the product or the service. For example, I ordered a salmon salad and requested no croutons because I eat gluten-free. The salad arrives and it's sprinkled with croutons. I kindly remind them of my intolerance and request, and the server rushed it back to the kitchen to make a fresh one… then they comp'd me to make up for the inconvenience of waiting, and they went above and beyond and gave me a free meal on a return visit. I was really wowed by how they rectified their mistake. Will I return? Of course. Now let me draw a bigger picture: What if I go back and the same thing happens? Salmon salad with croutons. I may think,

"Awesome. Another free meal and coupon." Only this time, the waiter apologizes, brings me the corrected salad 20 minutes later, and then that's it. No comp'd meal; no coupon… no consistency. I'm mad because they'd set the expectation of really great customer service on my first visit.

My story is hypothetical; however, this scenario plays out in plenty of small businesses. They don't have a system for handling mistakes. They're making it up as they go along. Depending on who you speak with or the kind of day they may be having determines the outcome. If this is how you're running your business right now, I bet you're losing customers and you don't even realize it.

Back to my story. Never forget that people talk to each other. What if I shared with plenty of folks that I'd been comp'd a meal and given a coupon to make up for the crouton error. I assure you, based on that level of customer service and solid attempt to rectify their error, I would happily share that… and recommend the restaurant! And what if the people I refer have a similar error without receiving the comp'd meal and coupon? They won't be happy, and when they share that information with me, I won't be happy and will stop referring.

Systems are simply the way I run my businesses. I know that it keeps things running smoothly and provides me with peace of mind and freedom. When my team knows what to do and how to do it, I don't need to be present. Someone asked me during an Instagram live when he should implement systems, after he shared he'd been in business for 12 years. The time to implement systems is: right now! If you're just getting started or have been running your business system-less for years, do it now.

Where to Start

You don't need to systemize every last thing, but you must certainly start by developing systems for client delivery and fulfillment. You want every client to get the same experience. Maybe you've never thought about what happens after product or service delivery, but you should. Stop and consider what experience you want clients to have after they buy. Will they get a confirmation email? What needs to be in that? Will someone personally reach out to them? Will they be added to an email sequence on how to use the product or to get excited to show up for the service? What about referrals? Do you have a system in place for existing customers and clients to refer others? Getting all of these components in place is the first system you should focus on.

However, I find most business owners start by incorporating systems that focus on marketing. I don't recommend that. The point of marketing is to drive more customers to your business. If you don't have solid systems in place for product and service delivery and follow-up, you are on your way to creating chaos. If your marketing works really well, but you can't deliver on the marketing promises, you're going to find yourself in trouble. Your customer service systems must be in place first! If you're crushing your marketing efforts and getting someone to purchase, you'll want them to purchase again, but if you can't deliver a consistent experience on the fulfillment side, the chance of a repeat sale falls dramatically. If you wow someone with your marketing, they'll expect a wow when they actually receive the product or service. You need to maintain the standard throughout the entire process.

Remember that it is harder to attract new customers than to get your existing customers to spend more and refer you. So why not put systems in place with existing customers to first give them a reason to stay with you and buy again and then rave about you to their friends and family? Only after you've put enough systems in place to give a five-star customer experience each and every time should you move on to marketing systems. There's no point in creating a killer marketing system if you can't serve your existing customer base and will struggle with more new customers coming through your door.

After refining your systems for customer service and delivery and marketing, then you can move on to focusing on operational systems, like accounting, HR, etc. That said, this order isn't carved in stone and shouldn't be a cookie cutter approach. When there's something that repeatedly causes stress, frustration, and chaos for you and your team, by all means prioritize creating a system to avoid repetition of the problem.

Strike a Balance

Of course I want you to systemize; however, I don't want you to overdo it. Put the systems in place that you absolutely need. I caution you against overdoing it because as you grow, chances are systems will break and will need to be revamped or at least tweaked. And you certainly don't need to create systems for things that have never happened yet. Build systems as you need them and then use them consistently. Take some time in thinking through the system as you're creating it, and put in the work to record or document it, so everyone on your team can implement the same way – consistently.

For example, don't create your interview process if you aren't going to hire for a while. I know that's common sense, but I've worked with some business owners who take this approach. When you decide to hire, take time to create your interview questions and save them for the next time you need to hire. Then as you grow, you won't be starting from scratch again.

> **Document your systems to avoid "recreating the wheel" every time.**

Also, make your systems a bit flexible and refine them as you go. I never had a system for terminating an employee until I had to terminate someone. When you're just getting started, you don't need to have every system in place immediately, but be sure to document them as you create them.

As I shared, the time to begin with systems is right now. This is not an advanced strategy that you'll only implement once your business is established. My own dedication to systems is the reason my businesses have always grown so fast. We put systems in place, and our customers love the experience and the consistency, so they keep coming back, and more importantly, they keep referring us!

Systems and Structure = Freedom

I've owned my performing arts schools now for over 20 years, and I used to work during our school-year opening week, greeting people and helping managing the craziness of returning and new students as we launched another year. There was a time when I ***had*** to be there for this, but I now have enough people trained that it's no longer on my plate. During one recent opening week, with my daughter now enrolled, I agreed to help on the night of her first class. I helped fitting dancers with shoes and escorting them to their classrooms. However, at this point, I'm not familiar with the software we're using, so I stay out of that. In fact, I happened to be at the front desk one time when our receptionist stepped away, and a mom came in to register her daughter. I was so embarrassed to admit that, although I was the owner, I didn't remember how to use the software! Thankfully, our receptionist returned quickly, and as I watched her enter all the details, it came back to me, and I realized it was the exact same system we'd set up years ago. I felt really proud that things were still running as if I was in the building all the time, and I still get goosebumps thinking about it.

I know that's what you want for your own business: having everything performed to your standards without you being the one doing it! This is why having systems and structure equals freedom –

your freedom. At a recent conference, when I shared that my two academies run themselves, another participant interrupted me: "Wait. They really run themselves? How?" I assured him it was true, and it was because I systemized. Yes, it's taken time, but it's completely worth the freedom I now enjoy.

When I started, I was a solopreneur for the first three years. I had systems... but they were in my head. When I hired two dance instructors and a receptionist, those systems were not helpful at all. And my own control-freak personality and worry about replicating things the way I would do them made me realize the importance of documenting systems and processes. Once I'd done that, it became easier to delegate, and the ability to delegate is a must if you ever plan to grow your business or take vacation or enjoy time off or have the business continue to run if you're otherwise unavailable.

Without a doubt, SOPs are the answer. However, creating processes is a process itself. You will not accomplish this in 30 days, nor should you try. As I already covered, you'll find the need to tweak as you go and as you grow. When clients tell me they want to be completely removed from their businesses, I typically recommend a three-year plan to get everything in place and running like a well-oiled operation. Yes, it can be done faster, and the speed depends completely on you and how much effort you're willing to put in and how dependent your business currently is on you.

So how do you go about creating and implementing systems? Here's the process:

1. Assign it. You can have others create systems for their own daily, weekly, monthly tasks, and you or their manager can approve it. Ensure the system is forward-looking, so it can be used for years. This is where your review (or that of a manager) comes into play. If you're just starting, you can assign it to yourself and mark time on your calendar each week to work on systems.
2. Document it. Whoever is creating the system should write down the steps or otherwise record it as video. Anything that's done via computer can be recorded as a video screen capture, making it easy for the next person to understand and follow the steps... consistently!
3. Test it. Ask someone who's unfamiliar with the task to read the instructions or watch the video to determine whether they can execute properly.

Here's a tip: Typically videos work better because you (or your manager) are actually going through the process, so it's unlikely that you are going to miss covering a step. This is also why it's important to test what you've documented.

Having read this chapter, I hope you can see how lacking SOPs is costing you time and money. Adding and documenting systems is not a quick task. It's an ongoing process, so start now! Again, start with your most pressing areas first, and don't over-systemize. Remember that you'll outgrow some systems over time, and you or a trusted manager should be putting the final stamp of approval on every SOP. Be open to continually tweaking and improving your systems, and you'll be on your way to having a well-oiled operation!

Creating Your Own Well-Oiled Operation

- Create standard operating procedures/systems for fulfillment first.
- Find the biggest frustrations in your business and create systems to fix them to avoid repeating the same errors or issues.
- Update any outdated systems or things that are no longer working.
- Have your key players get systems out of their heads and properly documented.
- Remember that video recording as instruction is probably the best way to capture all steps.
- Have someone else test the system.
- You or a manager you trust should put your stamp of approval on everything.

How would you score yourself right now on SOPs?

- Red: We have very few systems in place or the ones we have are not used consistently.

- Yellow: Some of this is in place but definitely still have some work to do.
- Green: Everyone on the team knows where to find documented SOPs and those are executed consistently, no matter who is handling it.

What needs to happen from this chapter? (Don't want to write in this book, download the workbook at www.welloiledoperations.com/bookbonuses)

Clean up: What can we remove?

_____
_____
_____
_____

Tighten up: What can we speed up?

_____
_____
_____
_____

Scale up: How can we plan for growth?

_____
_____
_____

Well-Oiled Operations^{TM}

_____
_____

To see a sample system, go to:
www.welloiledoperations.com/bookbonuses

SOPs

Chapter Nine:
Delegation & Ownership

I used to be a huge fan of HGTV and might still be although I don't watch much TV any longer. If you aren't familiar with the network, someone's usually renovating or buying a home. The designer, contractor, or real estate agent asks for a wish list. The would-be home buyer says she wants four bedrooms, a separate office, three bathrooms, open floor plan, an insane master suite along with the biggest closet you've ever seen, a great yard, and of course, in a nice neighborhood. When asked for the budget, the answer is "$150,000." I'd be yelling at the TV: "Lady, you're delusional!" even before the host could try to instill a sense of reality in the home buyer.

It's easy to see from the outside, but when you're in the middle of things, unrealistic expectations aren't so obvious. I see this happen in business all the time. Entrepreneurs are looking for unicorn team members who can do all sorts of things, mind reading included. When I ask for the salary range, it's down near or at minimum wage. (I do not yell at my clients that they're delusional, but it's the same thing!) Expectations and reality are clearly misaligned. The CEO has expectations that are too high. They think, "I hired this person to handle social media, and she still needs my help. I don't get it. Shouldn't she know how to do that? Now she wants me to pay $25/month for her to get coaching on Instagram. I thought she knew Instagram." Any of this sound familiar?

You have two options when it comes to hiring:
1. Hire entry-level. You'll pay the lower end of the salary scale, and you'll be the one to train and mold this person and provide the education they need.
2. Pay more and hire someone who already knows what they're doing and knows more than you.

Most CEOs merge the two – pay a lower salary but expect the new hire to be smarter than they are and not need any support. This is another form of delusion.

I'm not suggesting you can't have high expectations; however, you have to give new hires the training and support (and your time to answer questions) they need if you want them to fly in the first 90 days. Take a look at those two options again. It's always a decision between time and money. Which do you have more of? Which do you prefer to spend right now? Caution: Answering "I don't want to spend either" is delusional thinking. Plain and simple.

> *For the rest of your entrepreneurial life, you'll always have to choose between money and time.*

In the beginning of my own journey, I had more time than money, so I went with option one. Today, the inverse is true for me, so I spend more for a more highly qualified person. I'll also admit, I was delusional. I hired at the lower end of the pay scale, didn't train them well, and then didn't trust them to make decisions, so they were always dependent on me. The receptionist would wait until I was available to get my answer before responding to a customer. A dance teacher had to get her music approved by me before she could move forward with choreography. If I was unavailable, everything ground to a halt. It was an exhausting time for everyone. I corrected that problem years ago. In fact, I was gone for two weeks recently, and when I returned, my general manager filled me in with a seven-minute conversation. She didn't have to wait for anything. The business ran smoothly without me – nothing to catch up on!

I want you to get to that point in your own well-oiled business. To do so, you need to get out of your own way, let go a little bit, and then let go a little bit more.

Eliminate (or at Least Reduce) Decisions

So how do you get team members to make decisions without you? Your goal should be that they don't have to. They simply follow the system and by doing so, most, if not all decisions are already made. It all comes back to systems. (Reread the previous chapter if you must. In fact, I purposefully and strategically placed this chapter right after the one on systems for a reason.) Without systems, you have inconsistency, whether with customer or team member experiences. Inconsistency leads to complaints. The goal is to put systems in place and hire people who can run those systems with the consistency your clients and team members desire.

But what happens when something invariably pops up that you didn't plan for nor do you have documented? Here's my secret that keeps my business running without me: I allow the manager to decide in the moment how to handle the issue based on our company values. She has permission to do so because the last thing anyone wants to hear is, "I'll have to ask and get back to you." When there's a problem, your clients want it fixed now. I even allow certain team members to credit someone's account to rectify an error. We actually allow all of our front desk staff to allow a credit of up to $100.00. We call it the "$100 Happiness Policy." Anything exceeding that amount requires approval, but knowing they have the ability to fix an issue helps them take more ownership. It's good customer service. You might worry that your team member could "give away the shop." Not if you have a system. My team doesn't abuse this. They use their judgment and document what they did and why.

That brings us to accountability. When you hold someone accountable, you'll get the results you want and you'll get them faster. People always think I find "unicorns," like I'm a unicorn magnet, and I just wave a wand and the best candidates and team members appear. Yeah, I wish it were that easy. Here's the real formula:

- Attract the right people, then
- Teach them to work your systems, then
- Hold them accountable

Follow these steps in order, and you'll find yourself being accused of also being a unicorn magnet. It all comes down to transferring responsibility. It's more than delegation. If you've tried to delegate before and failed, I know the reason is that there was no true ownership. You might have assigned a task or project but there was no accountability. So how do you correct that?

Here are the four phases of delegation that includes transferring responsibility:

- Stage 1: Follow my system exactly.
- Stage 2: Create the system, and I'll approve, deny, or modify.
- Stage 3: Make a decision, and we'll discuss it at our next meeting and finalize a new system.
- Stage 4: I trust you to make the best decision for the company and create a new system.

Think about the person to whom you want to transfer responsibility. What phase are they in right now? They might be new and be at #1 or have been with you for years and are at #4. It's important for your team members to know where they are to avoid confusion and frustration for everyone.

Many of my clients have team members who don't know which phase they're in. Think about your own team. Do they know they have the authority to make a decision… and that you'll stand behind it? I was guilty of acting like I trusted them, but when I learned their decision, I made them feel like it was the wrong one – before I had systems in place. My manager called me out on it: "If you want me to run this company and not interrupt you in the moment, you need to be fine with my decision." And she was right. We decided she had authority to make decisions in the moment to serve the client, and we would discuss and build a system after the fact.

If your values are important, and not just fluff, they'll serve as the guide for all of your team members to make decisions. Communicate that to them. Allow for a learning curve, and you'll find that before long, they'll be making the same decisions you would – as long as you have systems in place. Without systems, we're back to inconsistency. Inconsistency derails expectations, both yours and those of your team members.

The more you let go and let your team members execute the system, the less you'll feel you need to micromanage. People will start to take ownership of their positions and outcomes because systems will provide confidence and they'll begin to feel a level of trust. Think back to the chapter on hiring and the need to cover the three key areas of any business: product mastery, marketing, and operations. Your goal is to get your team to take ownership of these.

Honestly, I've seen "leadership teams" that have no leaders. Why? The CEO continually steps in. You will never fully be out of the day-to-day operations if you are still running one or all of these departments. It may feel impossible to offload these, so start with one. Give people on your team a chance to shine. I'm sure you have someone right now who wishes they had more responsibility. Team members want to feel important, valued, and trusted. It's time to delegate properly and transfer ownership with accountability.

The End Game

You cannot decide to put systems in place because you anticipate getting out of the business in 30, 60, or even 90 days. It takes time. If you want a sellable business when you decide to retire, you need to start today! Without having a well-oiled operation, you will very likely never get the money you think your business is worth when it comes time to sell it.

Actually, I build sellable businesses even though I have no intention of selling anytime soon. You have to keep the end in mind. Even when I built my house, I made decisions based on selling it. Before we moved in, I was building to sell it. We built at a time bathtubs were falling out of favor for big walk-in showers. I told my husband we needed both, and he reminded me I never take baths. I didn't care. The next buyer might want a tub. (And now, I really love baths!)

I'll wrap up this chapter returning to HGTV and the show *Love It or List It*. Couples simultaneously fix up a problem home while shopping for a new one. One always wants to fix it and stay and the other wants to list it and leave. In the end, the previous problems are resolved, the old place is beautiful, and many choose to stay. Plus, they've kept the end game in focus to create a more sellable asset if they choose to list it. Both spouses are happy in the end.

That's what I want for you in building your business. Fix the problems and create a well-oiled operation and enjoy it while you're running it and then have a really valuable asset to sell for top dollar when you're ready to move on. A sellable business is fun and enjoyable to run because it doesn't need you!

Creating Your Own Well-Oiled Operation

- What is your greater resource right now: time or money? You will always have to choose between those two.
- Hire people who will work your systems.
- Ensure accountability and follow ups are happening to ensure systems are being executed properly.
- Give your team latitude to make decisions, based on your systems and company values.
- Delegation requires ownership or it never works.
- Your values (as long as they're not fluff) serve as the guide for decision-making and ownership. Communicate them!
- Team members want to feel important, valued, and trusted. Give them a chance to shine.

How would you score yourself right now on delegation?

- Red: No leaders nor true leaders with ownership.
- Yellow: Some of this is in place but definitely still have some work to do.
- Green: We have all three departments (fulfillment, marketing, operations) with true leaders and the CEO no longer "owns" any of them.

What needs to happen from this chapter? (Don't want to write in this book, download the workbook at www.welloiledoperations.com/bookbonuses)

Clean up: What can we remove?
_____
_____
_____
_____
_____

Tighten up: What can we speed up?
_____
_____
_____
_____
_____

Scale up: How can we plan for growth?
_____
_____
_____
_____
_____

For a short video on how I delegate, go to www.welloiledoperations.com/bookbonuses

Chapter Ten:

Leverage

Think back to the beginning of the book. I asked you to determine where you are today: Pioneer, Pathfinder, Powerplayer, or Powerhouse. I recommend you step into the role of Powerhouse ***right now***. If you want a well-oiled operation that runs without you, make the decision and start acting like a Powerhouse now. Don't procrastinate any longer, or you'll find yourself a year or more down the road in the exact place you are right now. Anything you postpone only gets harder to correct later. Start acting like a Powerhouse.

That said and in wrapping up, I want you to understand the concept of leverage. When I think of that word, I also think of the word "advantage." But leverage only becomes an advantage if you use it properly. Think about getting the most out of what you have. Don't focus on what you lack. That negative focus is exactly why businesses get stuck. We teach our clients to lean in to what's working and build on that.

There are five areas that you can begin leveraging today: time, money, team, Best Sellers, and Best Clients. Let's look at each one.

Leveraging Time

You cannot have this year's calendar look like last year's calendar or you are simply going to get last year's results. This was a mind-blowing revelation to one of my clients recently. He really believed he had his calendar dialed in and was only doing the things no one else on his team could do. While that sounds okay, I'll tell you the truth: If you want to scale, at some point the things "only you can do" must go on someone else's plate. I'm sure they're big things, like leading team meetings, working with clients, being the face of your marketing, and executing on CEO-level tasks; however, it is possible to delegate these very high-level activities.

If you want more from your business (with less time and effort from you) but your calendar hasn't changed in a while, it's time to reassess what you are doing with your time. If you haven't done a time audit yet, do it now.

At a conference, I had a conversation with Todd Herman, a high-performance coach, and he really opened my eyes about my own schedule and how I wasn't leveraging my time very well. At the time, I pretty much spent my week with back-to-back appointments, either with my team or clients, or I was recording a podcast as well as being interviewed on someone else's. I thought I had dialed in my activities, but he pointed out that I had no time in my calendar to be the visionary. He said, "Think about the show *Modern Family*. They record an entire season in a few months, then they all take off. Every sport has an off-season to recharge. You don't have an off-season. You are going all-out all the time." He was right, and it clicked, so I've restructured my days:

- Mondays: Internal meetings and coaching inside Well-Oiled Operations™ Mastery for one hour.

- Tuesdays: Wide open and end with a massage.
- Wednesdays: Mornings are open; coaching my Powerhouse Mastermind in the afternoon.
- Thursdays: External appointments, including podcast interviews, social lives, meeting with contractors, CPA, etc. (I admit that I dread Thursdays a bit because it's usually back-to-back, but that used to be my schedule Mondays through Fridays. At least now, it's only Thursdays!)
- Fridays: Wide open, so my last appointment on Thursday feels like the weekend. Some weeks, I use Fridays to catch up; some weeks, I enjoy a three-day weekend to recharge.

I know it can be difficult to rein in your time and re-adjust your schedule because you'll probably need to spend more time initially in order to step away. Years ago, I started spending more time in the studio with my teaching staff. I purchased a curriculum and paid for them to attend a two-day training in Chicago to learn from its founder. I spent extra time (and money) to ensure my teachers were fully capable before I stepped away. When I stepped away from teaching, I then stepped into the office and set up systems and trained those team members before I backed away from that. Yes, it took more of my time, but it was a temporary sacrifice to achieve the long-term result I now enjoy. If you procrastinate because you don't want to spend the time now, it will simply never happen, and you will forever be spending time in your business rather than enjoying greater freedom.

Leveraging Money

Yes, you have to spend money to make money, and I'm all for investing in my business but highly against wasting money. I constantly ask: Is this an expense or a revenue-generating investment? For example, are you buying a new iPhone and writing it off as a business expense even though you have the second most-recent version and it works pretty much the same? If so, it's an expense. Before you argue and tell me the latest version has a better camera and you're shooting videos for marketing, so it's technically a revenue generator, I want you to think about how much ***additional revenue*** you gained because your videos are now the tiniest bit clearer.

Don't make the mistake that a lot of business owners make, taking "write offs" while it's driving their profit margins down. It's one thing to spring for the new iPhone (or whatever purchase you want) if your bank account is sitting pretty and your profit margins are at the high end for your industry. It's another story if you're barely breaking even. To leverage your money, instead of purchasing the latest gadget, it's always better to invest in your team, hire a coach, or join a program that will truly deliver a noticeable return on your investment. I recently invested in a new coaching program that doubled my investment in 30 days. A new iPhone will never do that.

When I first started my business, I was very frugal, including personal expenses. My friends would spend $15.00 to go to a movie, and I'd pass and save the money for my business. Many might think, "What's $15.00? That won't make a difference." But it does and every little bit adds up. We lived modestly and it paid off, so we're at a point now where we don't need to be so frugal. That would not have happened so quickly if we'd spent differently earlier. Social media is creating a lot of "keep up with the Joneses" mindset, and people are overspending on things others can see and cutting expenses in places they shouldn't in order to pay for it. We recently had a consultation with a prospect who was a perfect fit for Well-Oiled Operations™ Mastery. Her business relied heavily on her being there and her right-hand manager couldn't make a decision without her. She was expecting and wanted to enjoy her maternity leave without being tied to her business. She didn't join our program because she "wasn't able to spend that kind of money right now," but her Instagram showed off her "babymoon" travel photos and plenty of other images that were not revenue generators. Sure, I bet her babymoon was relaxing, but you know what wasn't? The maternity leave she never really got because she couldn't step away from her business.

Right now, I want you to take a look at your last credit card statement. Look at every single purchase and categorize them as expense or revenue generator. Be honest or you're only fooling yourself. Get in the habit of asking before every single purchase: expense or revenue generator?

Leverage Team

When clients start to drink my Kool-Aid, they want to hire a lot of people. They frequently ask, "Who should I hire next?" I want you to think about your team in a different way, based on what we just covered about leveraging money... and it may be harsh. Some people on your team are revenue generators, but some of them are expenses. Let that sink in, and I'm willing to bet you already know who's which.

Take a moment to assess every one of your team members. If you're seeing someone as an expense, put them on a time audit to uncover how they are really spending their day. When that audit confirms their role as an expense, develop a plan of action to turn them into a revenue generator. Yes, someone who's an expense can become a revenue generator, but they will need your help. Don't place the blame on them. Take responsibility for the "expense" tasks to which they've been assigned, and now change those tasks so that person is contributing to revenue and profit. For example, the receptionist may have the task of answering the phone and greeting customers, but the way that's handled can make a huge difference! Provide the training needed. With a change in responsibilities (and ownership), they can be producing revenue in as few as 90 days... maybe sooner.

For your existing revenue generators, what have you done to acknowledge them lately? Everyone wants a pat on the back. Send them a text or acknowledge in person how much you appreciate their efforts and results. If you have an expense team member you decide to let go, could you hire an assistant for your revenue generator, so that together they contribute even more to your bottom line?

For almost every small business, payroll is the biggest line item on the financial sheet. You simply cannot afford payroll as an expense rather than an investment. Have you looked at each position's salary and calculated how much revenue they generate for it? If someone works part-time for you at $25,000/year, you have to determine how much revenue their work generated. The answer must be greater than $25,000. Most business owners don't do this calculation.

On the flip side, be careful that you aren't overpaying your revenue producers. I've seen plenty of bonus structures that have gotten out of hand and old commission rates that don't make sense any longer. Make sure you are spending your payroll dollars wisely. We have a base rate with commissions and incentives built in, and I make sure those incentives are working to hit the bottom line. This way, both my team members and the company win when they succeed. I want to share the wealth with my revenue producers, and I stay focused on ensuring every position is filled with a revenue producer.

Leverage Best Sellers

What's working in your business? Or what used to work? Success leaves tracks and clues, but you have to look for them. Ask yourself (and your team): What sells best and why? Is it the name, the price, the offer, or the messaging? What attracts customers and how can we lean into that? Look for those success clues and then repeat.

If you hold on to something that isn't selling, you take focus off what is. When I have a new idea I think is going to be big, I admit that it's hard to let go when I realize I missed the mark and no one wants it. My ego wants to keep fighting to continue with it, trying to figure out a better angle to market it. What really happens is that I'm stealing time away from what already sells. That said, you have to find the happy medium. There will always be someone who's selling something new and then quickly changing up their offer without giving it enough time to even test the messaging or perhaps refine the offer to make it successful. And there will always be someone who holds on to something that's not working for months (or even years). Continue to place ***most of your focus*** on the thing that is bringing in revenue right now while you determine if you should continue to pursue a new product or service.

For instance, let's say you make candles. You started out with a stand at the farmers' market and business boomed and you want to grow, so maybe you consider picture frames. You think it makes sense. Most people buy candles as gifts, and frames make great gifts too, so why not? Plus, another revenue stream sounds great. But the frames don't take off like the candles, so you double down on your marketing efforts. You get different styles and colors, but they still don't sell, and you're racking your brain trying to figure out how to move them. At some point, you offer them at clearance and call it a day. So what? You lost a little bit of money on the inventory. No big deal, right? Wrong. You must consider the lost opportunity cost that accompanies your lack of focus on selling candles – the best seller that grew your business to start. What if you'd sold three candles instead of one because you were trying to sell a frame as well? As you're reading this, it's easy to see the error. I can spot this all the time with my clients. It's easy because it's not your business and it's not your ego that was tied to the idea. This is magnified when your ideal client agrees with the product expansion… but then they don't buy. Sell more of what's already selling.

Leverage Best Clients

All clients are not created equal. There are some who are a dream to work with and there are some who cause a pit in your stomach when you see their name pop up. You know exactly what I'm talking about. The problem is that we tend to focus on the loudest person. They make their complaints known, and then we "fix" our programs, products, or services to serve them. In doing so, we might well be making changes our best clients *don't* want. Ultimately, bad behavior annoys our best clients and may even cause them to leave! I'll be honest: I've done this more times than I'd like to admit. But I'm much better now. In fact, I just "fired" a Powerhouse client because I know what happens if you don't, and yes, one bad apple can spoil the bunch.

I learned this at my studio. If you've ever seen the show *Dance Moms*, you've seen some crazy behavior displayed by grown women. I'd like to tell you it's complete fiction, but I've seen some of that kind of behavior in our studio from time to time. We had one of those moms, and her behavior was intolerable. We eventually showed her the door, but it was too late. The damage was done, and we'd lost a few of our best clients because they didn't want to deal with her. And these folks didn't return even after the crazy mom left. They'd found a new place and didn't want to switch again.

Do an audit of your clients to leverage them, just like you did an audit of your team members. Who spends the most? Who pays on time? Who's an ambassador for your company? Do what you can to determine why this person is one of your best clients and do what you can to replicate attracting more like them.

You don't need many new strategies to improve and grow your business. You simply need to leverage and get better at these five areas to see massive results. What if, over the next five months, you focused on one area each month – time, money, team, Best Sellers, and Best Clients. Imagine how different your business could be five months from now!

Creating Your Own Well-Oiled Operation

- Keeping the same activities on your calendar (no matter how disciplined you are) will get you the same results.

- Before you spend money, ask if it's an expense or a revenue generator.
- Each team member is either an expense or a revenue generator. Turn the former into the latter or it's time to let them go.
- Sell more of what's already selling.
- Never allow bad clients to ruin your best clients' experience, either directly or indirectly because you've mistakenly altered your program, product, or service.

How would you score yourself right now on leverage?
- Red: We are not leveraging what we currently have.
- Yellow: Some of this is in place but definitely still have some work to do.
- Green: We are constantly refining and improving the areas of time, money, team, Best Sellers, and Best Clients.

What needs to happen from this chapter? (Don't want to write in this book, download the workbook at www.welloiledoperations.com/bookbonuses)

Clean up: What can we remove?
_____
_____
_____

_____
_____

Tighten up: What can we speed up?

_____
_____
_____
_____

Scale up: How can we plan for growth?

_____
_____
_____
_____

Don't forget that we have so many more free templates, bonus trainings, and more at www.welloiledoperations.com/bookbonuses

Bonus Chapter:
Quick Start Guide

It's easy to gain inspiration from reading a book, but it's entirely different to be moved to implement. I know you have the best intentions and want to do what's best for your business, but it's almost always easier said than done.

For that reason, I'm including a Quick Start Guide, so you can get the most out of this book. As I mentioned at the beginning, I encourage you to have each person on your leadership team read the book, and meet regularly (weekly or bi-weekly) to discuss each chapter. But don't miss the critical step: Before moving to the next chapter, meet again and determine what and how you will implement what you learned from the current chapter.

For those who want to go faster with greater accountability and mindset shifts and want to go deeper into what I've covered, I encourage you to check out our great Well-Oiled Operations™ Mastery program by visiting: www.WellOiledOperations.com. One of the beauties of this program is that your leadership team is invited to go through the program with you. If you want to motivate your team and really light them up, this is the program to do just that. I'd love to help you implement and get your business running without you, so you can take that well-deserved vacation, enjoy your evenings and weekends, and never miss an important family event again.

Remember that things go well... until they don't. When that happens, I urge you to return to these pages and reassess as needed in each category. What got you here won't get you there, and at some point, the people who were right for your business three years ago may not be the right people to help you get to the next level. As we scale, we break the things that worked, so that means it's time to repeat the process. I hope this book becomes one you'll refer to often and that you'll continue to implement what you learn from it.

If you're like me, you like a checklist, so here are a few key action items from each phase.

Phase 1 – Well-Oiled Strategic Planning: Roadmap, Prioritization, Maximizing ROI

- ❏ Create or refine your org chart.
- ❏ Define company values that you use to hire, fire, and everything in between.
- ❏ Condense all these important details into your Same Pager™.
- ❏ Assign KPIs and critical numbers.
- ❏ Weekly reports from appropriate team members.
- ❏ Write out your three-year vision and share it with the team.
- ❏ Start maximizing your project management software.
- ❏ Determine projects versus routines for each team member.
- ❏ Assign the 5-Hour Challenge to increase efficiencies.

- ☐ Incorporate time audits every 90 days.

Phase 2 – Well-Oiled Leadership: Effective Team Meetings, Better Boundaries & Communication, Solid Foundations, Hiring & Firing

- ☐ Set up a meeting structure and rhythm for your entire team.
- ☐ Assess where you are allowing bad boundaries to happen and with whom.
- ☐ Decide what would you like any relationship to look like and be clear with each person.
- ☐ Remind the team of the org chart and who they should be contacting with questions, etc.
- ☐ Onboard all current team members who were never properly onboarded when hired.
- ☐ Create proper documents and contracts, and require signatures by team members.
- ☐ Figure out your weakest department and assign someone to own it.
- ☐ Refine your hiring process to incorporate "hoops" and sample projects to weed out unqualified candidates.
- ☐ Find a professional in your state/country who can give you legal advice about terminations.
- ☐ Start Performance Improvement Plans if necessary.

Phase 3 – Well-Oiled Systems: SOPs, Delegation & Ownership, Leverage

- ❏ Create standard operating procedures/systems for fulfillment first, then marketing, then operations.
- ❏ Find your biggest frustrations in your business and create systems to fix them.
- ❏ Update any outdated systems or things that are no longer working.
- ❏ Make sure to have someone else test the systems to ensure instructions are clear.
- ❏ You or a manager you trust should be putting the stamp of approval on all SOPs.
- ❏ Hire people who will work your systems and fire people who refuse to do so.
- ❏ Make sure accountability and follow-up is happening to ensure systems are executed properly.
- ❏ Before you spend more money, ask yourself, "Is this an expense or a revenue generator?"
- ❏ Sell more of what is already selling.
- ❏ Fire any clients who are ruining your best clients' experience with your business.

Don't let the list overwhelm you. Remember: one step at a time. If you follow this checklist, you'll get quick wins in each phase. I've seen clients experience positive results in as little as one week.

If you feel paralyzed by this list, go to www.WellOiledOperations.com to learn how we can help you tackle this one step at a time. We'll hold you accountable and we'll be there to coach you when you get stuck, when a team members challenges you, or when you don't know how to determine an expense or revenue generator.

Promise me one thing: You'll do this consistently for 90 days as a test. Within that time, you should already feel a shift in clarity, focus, and even results. Those results may be people finishing their weekly tasks, realizing KPIs are off (too high, too low), and seeing even a small increase in your bank account and bottom line. With even the slightest bit of progress, keep going and do another 90-day test. With the second round, things will massively click for the right people.

Return to this book to "rinse and repeat" as needed. The more you read it, the more you'll grasp. It will take time. You can't judge the work out if you didn't show up at the gym! Well-Oiled Operations™ works, but only if you work it.

Quick Start Guide

Resources

Be sure to head over to: www.welloiledoperations.com/bookbonuses and get the following for your business:

- See our Same PagerTM
- Get the companion workbook
- Find a list of potential company values
- See our favorite project management software programs
- KPI tracking spreadsheet
- 5-Hour Challenge
- 1:1 Meeting Agenda
- Scripts to establish boundaries
- Get your Scale Score
- Listen to a bonus training with DEI expert, Rhoda Moret: "Diversity Advantages in the Workplace"
- Review sample systems
- Watch my delegation video
- Free templates, bonus training, and more

Stacy's Bookshelf

Here is a collection of the books I've referred to in these pages:

E-myth Revisited: Why Most Small Businesses Don't Work and What to Do About It by Michael Gerber

Resources

Good to Great by Jim Collins

The Great Game of Business by Jack Stack

Profit First by Mike Michalowicz

Key Performance Indicators (KPI): The 75 measures every manager needs to know by Bernard Marr

Traction: Get a Grip on Your Business by Gino Wickman

Never Lose a Customer Again: Turn Any Sale into Lifelong Loyalty in 100 Days by Joey Coleman

Acknowledgments

Team Foot Traffic: It is a privilege to work with you each and every day. Seeing each of you continually grow has been so beautiful to watch. Having our clients reference you all as unicorns and saying, "I need a Sarah," "Where do I find a Cara?" and "What did you post to attract Bella?" warms my heart. You are world class and make work so fun and enjoyable.

Team APA: The only reason I am able to do what I do every day is because of the extraordinary talent we have at APA. To my sister, Jamie Cook, who holds it all together and runs the business as her own, I am so grateful to have you. To our amazing directors, Tiffany and Garrett, I trust you 100 percent. You love what you do and always play full out. You have attracted the most incredible people to join us in our mission. Grateful for each and every one of you!

Thank you to my editor, Ann Deiterich for putting the finishes touches on the book and bringing it to life.

Thank you to Jim Saurbaugh for designing a beautiful cover.

To my parents and grandparents: I had no idea what a blessing it would be to grow up in a family small business. Watching you raise us and the business at the same time has taught me so much about how I wanted to build my business and raise my family. Thank you for a once-in-a-lifetime opportunity.

To Kent, Tanner and Teagan: I love our family so much. You are the reason I want to create a Well-Oiled Operation so that we can spend as much time together and all be present with one another. I love our family dinners, vacations in Florida, and camping in our RV. Your love and support is more than I could ever ask for. You never make me feel guilty for getting my work done or taking another work trip. Love you!

About the Author

Stacy Tuschl has made a name for herself as an expert in growing small businesses. Put it this way: Stacy started her own business at the age of 18 in her parents' backyard and turned that company into a multi-million-dollar business she still runs today. (The Academy of Performing Arts has two locations in her home state of Wisconsin.) In addition to being a Small Business Growth Coach, Stacy is a best-selling author and founder of Well-Oiled Operations™ Mastery – helping small businesses around the world get more customers in the door, more profit in their pocket, and more happiness in their homes.

When local area businesses started asking Stacy how she grew her company so rapidly, it sparked the inspiration needed to launch the *Well-Oiled Operations*™ podcast. Her podcast now has over two million downloads and is frequently on the top 30 of all management podcasts on iTunes. She's interviewed leading experts like Suze Orman, Dave Hollis, Jasmine Star, and Amy Porterfield.

Stacy was named the 2019 Wisconsin Small Business Person of the Year by the United States Small Business Administration. She was featured in *Inc. Magazine* as one of the top 10 podcasts for moms looking to grow a thriving business and has also been featured in the *Huffington Post* and popular podcasts like *Online Marketing Made Easy with Amy Porterfield*, *Eventual Millionaire*, and *Social Media Marketing*.

Stacy lives in Milwaukee, Wisconsin with her husband, Kent, and daughters, Tanner and Teagan.

Made in United States
Troutdale, OR
07/16/2024